AGAINST CIVILITY

AGAINST CIVILITY

The Hidden Racism in Our Obsession with Civility

ALEX ZAMALIN

BEACON PRESS
BOSTON

BEACON PRESS
Boston, Massachusetts
www.beacon.org

Beacon Press books
are published under the auspices of
the Unitarian Universalist Association of Congregations.

24 23 22 21   8 7 6 5 4 3 2 1

This book is printed on acid-free paper that meets the uncoated paper
ANSI/NISO specifications for permanence as revised in 1992.

Text design and composition by Kim Arney

Library of Congress Cataloging-in-Publication Data
Names: Zamalin, Alex, author.
Title: Against civility : the hidden racism in our obsession
with civility / Alex Zamalin.
Description: Boston : Beacon Press, [2021] | Includes
bibliographical references and index.
Identifiers: LCCN 2020022047 (print) | LCCN 2020022048 (ebook) |
ISBN 9780807026540 (hardcover) | ISBN 9780807026564 (ebook)
Subjects: LCSH: Racism—United States—History. | Courtesy—Political
aspects—United States—History. | Political culture—United
States—History. | Equality—United States—History. | Protest
movements—United States—History. | United States—Race relations—History.
Classification: LCC E184.A1 Z355 2021 (print) | LCC E184.A1 (ebook) |
DDC 305.800973—dc23
LC record available at https://lccn.loc.gov/2020022047
LC ebook record available at https://lccn.loc.gov/2020022048

For Alison, Sam, and Anita

CONTENTS

Chapter 1

CIVILITY HAS NEVER BEEN NEUTRAL IN ITS USES AND IMPACTS

From the moment he launched his presidential campaign in the summer of 2015 by descending an escalator in New York's Trump Tower, Republican Donald Trump decisively rejected the rules of public decorum for politicians. He unapologetically called Mexicans rapists and proposed a total shutdown of Muslim immigration to the United States. He wouldn't denounce the white supremacists—such as David Duke, former Grand Wizard of the Louisiana Ku Klux Klan—who had endorsed him. And so he emboldened hardened racists who felt stiffed after eight years under a black president to speak their minds, bringing all their venom that lurked just below the surface of American society back into the mainstream. In a nonstop barrage of tweets, he hurled personal insults against his opponents. Women were subject to sexist tirades about their bodies, disabled people were mocked, and asylum seekers characterized as mass murderers.

Although many of his statements were lies, to his loyal supporters, Trump was a truth-teller of the first order. But to his critics, he was the most dangerous political figure ever to get so close to power. During the presidential campaign, many media pundits convinced themselves Trump was a bad dream, a reality TV actor and failed businessman who was just temporarily basking in the spotlight to make an extra buck and trying to bolster his ego and quench his insatiable thirst for power. Nothing could have prepared them for November 4, 2016, when the unbelievable happened: Trump was elected over Democrat Hillary Clinton and would soon become the forty-fifth president of the United States.

Total dread soon turned into mass defiance. On January 21, 2017, the day after Trump's inauguration, millions of people across the world protested his presidency. In the US, the Women's March in Washington, DC, drew almost five hundred thousand people, and in big cities and small towns, estimates suggested that anywhere from three to five million people joined affiliated demonstrations. Women organized the march, but it became a rallying cry for all those opposing Trump's far-right policy vision of gender and racial inequality, environmental degradation, and economic privatization. Eventually, participants in the march, and those who supported it, called themselves the "Resistance" to Trump's presidency. This diverse group of protesters didn't agree on everything. Some thought Trump's electoral college victory violated democratic principles; others worried about Russian meddling in the 2016 US elections; some were afraid of Trump's authoritarianism, while others saw in his victory a continuation of thirty years of reactionary presidencies from Richard M. Nixon to Ronald Reagan to George W. Bush. But there was one thing of which every member of the Resistance was certain: Trump didn't represent their views, and they would fight his agenda.

As the days became months and months became years, a consensus narrative has emerged: to combat Trump and the divisiveness that his presidency has spurred, we need to be more civil with one another. Everywhere you look—the *New York Times*, CNN, National Public Radio—pundits, journalists, and best-selling authors prescribe this antidote to our infighting. The center-right *Times* op-ed columnist David Brooks said, "I think we've gotten out of the habit of talking about what is good character and what is good morality."[1] Shortly after Trump was elected, the black liberal CNN commentator Van Jones remarked, "Hopefully [Trump's election] will open up our eyes to how fragile democracy is and how key civility is to civilization. Civility isn't just some optional value in a multicultural, multistate democratic republic. Civility is the key to civilization."[2] In July 2017, an NPR/Marist College poll found that seven out of ten Americans believed civility between Washington politicians had declined since Trump took office, and only 6 percent believed the tone had improved in the same time period.[3]

We're told that the most effective way to oppose Trump and save the soul of our nation is to be politer, less rancorous and embittered, more compassionate and rule-abiding, more responsible in our choices and empathetic in our dialogue. Don't be too disruptive or unruly in the streets. Play by the rules of the game. Look to compromise when you can. Don't rock the boat. Don't be too loud. Stop being so angry. Listen to the police and obey their orders. Follow the law at all times.

Invocations to be more civil are directed toward both sides of the political aisle. Civility is recruited to criticize the rhetoric of both white supremacists—characterized by the white nationalist rally in Charlottesville, Virginia, in 2017 and the rise of the racist alt-right—and Movement for Black Lives (also known as Black Lives Matter) protesters. Civility is said to be lacking in activists toppling Confederate statues in the South and in students occupying university buildings, as hundreds did at the University of Vermont in February 2018 to push for more inclusive and anti-racist administrative policies, or as Howard University students did in April of that year to push for more affordable housing on campus. And civility is invoked when college administrators and professors denounce the culture of political correctness in their defense of free speech and academic expertise. As the current president of Wesleyan University, historian Michael S. Roth, recently asserted in a blog post, "Name-calling or assuming the status of the victimized is among the least productive forms of disagreement. Outrage may lead to feelings of solidarity, but it insulates us from the possibility of changing our minds, from opening our thinking . . . Citizens must avoid falling into the tired tropes of both callout culture and accusations of political correctness."[4]

Also implored to be more civil are professional athletes, such as former San Francisco 49ers quarterback Colin Kaepernick or National Football League defensive back Malcolm Jenkins, who take a knee or raise clenched fists during the national anthem before sporting events to oppose systemic racism. And so are those who loudly decry them as unpatriotic and demand for the immediate restoration of a besmirched national honor.

Civility is beneficial for a society beset by extremism, say political observers who claim the center and define themselves against the fringe. As liberal democratic norms wane across the globe—with the rise of far-right authoritarian, anti-immigrant regimes in Poland, Hungary, Brazil, and the Philippines, and the growing popularity of political parties like Alternative for Germany (AFD) or the National Rally (formerly the National Front led by Marine Le Pen) in France—civility appeals to the mainstream because it conjures a common ground, a nonpolitical arena where agreement isn't too far away, where consensus is within reach, where moderation counters aggression, where reason trumps the irrational.

Nowhere is this truer than when it comes to race. Because de jure racial segregation was abolished with *Brown v. Board of Education of Topeka, Kansas*; landmark civil rights legislation of the 1960s was passed; and the first black president, Barack Obama, was twice elected, there is the feeling among centrist Democrats, Republicans, and independents that—despite Trump's dangerous rise and the white nationalist elements he has unleashed—civility is indispensable for progress. Equality can be incrementally expanded only if Obama's legacy—of signing into law the Affordable Care Act of 2010, of increasing aid to community colleges, of trying to incrementally reduce mass incarceration, of diminishing the pay gap between men and women, and of reaching across the aisle—is remembered and reaffirmed. And only by these incremental measures can we achieve freedom for all. The underlying thinking can be boiled down to this: Yes, Trump won, but only because elements of the white working class who tended to vote Democrat were swayed by his false promises and because so many others, utterly unenthused and disgusted by the incivility on both sides, stayed home. We must therefore double down on what former First Lady Michelle Obama said, which was echoed by Democratic presidential candidate Hillary Clinton during the 2016 election: "When they go low, we go high."

Civility is seen as the platform on which to build a winning Democratic coalition. We heard it from the House Democrats, newly empowered with their fresh majority after the 2018 midterm elections, when, led by Speaker Nancy Pelosi, they talked about "being the adults in the room." The slate of centrist Democratic candidates for president—Joe Biden, Cory Booker, Pete Buttigieg, Amy Klobuchar, Kamala Harris, and Beto O'Rourke—promised a return to a saner, gentler, less divisive, and healthier time.

In the Democratic Party today, civility is a more cheery and populist, less technocratic and expert-driven, more sensible and less conservative update of Arkansas-governor-turned-president Bill Clinton's 1990s strategy of triangulation, which involved forming a coalition of law-and-order voters, fiscal conservatives, and traditional liberals. Moderate Democrats in particular believe the path to reclaiming relevancy is about gathering under one tent disaffected white Republican-voting never-Trump suburbanites and an increasingly diverse base of nonwhites and progressives, women, and working people.

Civility sounds like a good thing. If we think about our daily lives and our relationships with neighbors and friends, the word suggests warmth and affection, forgiveness and humility—and good manners—things to which we should aspire. In truth, most people don't want to come off as rude or impolite at a dinner party, on the sidewalk, or on the street corner.

But politics isn't everyday life. Politics is about organizing the competing interests within a community, distributing socioeconomic resources, making determinations about whose lives matter and whose don't. Politics is about parties struggling to win elections, social movements trying to press the ruling class for greater freedom, politicians signing bills into laws that affect how much we pay in taxes, who ends up going to jail, and what kinds of schools our children go to. This is an arena of power and struggle.

Once we think about politics in this way, we need to ask ourselves this: Does civility take us one step closer to our goal of liberation for all people? Does it sway politicians to make sweeping changes in public policy? Is it something to which we should aspire in public life as we do with our friends and neighbors?

We can speculate about these questions abstractly. But the best way to answer them is by looking to similar struggles in the past. History teaches us what has worked and what hasn't. It is a record of success and failure from which we have much to learn. This book's purpose is to track the history of the relationship between civility and antiblack racism in the United States to see what lessons it might have for us today.

When we do this, a clear picture emerges, as surprising as it is unsettling. Civility is a central term through which racial inequality has been maintained. Civility is exalted in the language of slaveholders, segregationists, lynch mobs, and eugenicists. It is also enshrined in the language of free marketeers and preachers of fiscal responsibility. And, surprisingly, it is elevated in the language of well-intentioned liberals, self-described moderates, and devout progressives. All of them traffic in ideas about public etiquette to declare what counts as good citizenship and what doesn't. From slavery to Jim Crow, to black ghettoization, to mass incarceration, to police brutality, the idea of civility has been enlisted to treat black suffering with apathy or to maintain an unjust status quo. Worse, it has been a tool for silencing dissent, repressing political participation, enforcing economic inequality, and justifying violence upon people of color.

Slaveholders touted their compassion for the enslaved, even as they crushed slave rebellions in the 1830s. Lynch mobs in the 1890s declared their chivalry for white women as the very reason for burning black people, who were seen as a public menace that sexually threatened white women. Free marketeers in the 1980s characterized poor people, especially poor black people, as lazy, and accused them of secretly exploiting the welfare system. As a result, in the 1990s, Democratic president Bill Clinton and the sitting Republican Congress, in what was hailed as a great moment of bipartisanship, ended welfare as we knew it. Contemporary attempts by conservatives to restrict the right to vote are based not only on the myth of voter fraud (which is virtually nonexistent) but on the idea that citizens need to be civically engaged enough to overcome any obstacles to voter registration. Policymakers who helped build our current system of mass incarceration talk about order and public safety.

And progressives interested in keeping the peace and behaving lawfully—as well as preserving their own socioeconomic privilege—have told anti-racist activists to slow down, to avoid creating too much instability, to keep their protests to a bare minimum. Although progressives have supported the struggle against racial injustice in ways their conservative counterparts never have, many aren't willing to topple the system by any means necessary. Some nineteenth-century antislavery reformers believed abolition would only work if they made moral appeals to white people's consciences. And many 1960s civil rights liberals thought any image of black lawlessness would threaten white sympathy for black Southerners toiling under Jim Crow.

The idea of civility has been recruited in these ways by these figures because it provides the perfect language for creating friends and identifying enemies, and for defining what is good and what is evil, legal and illegal, right and wrong. Civility avoids moral gray areas and offers something more cleanly defined but also less complex. This is suitable for those who want to demonize their opponents but also want to characterize themselves as virtuous.

At the same time, civility is an effective way to distract. Saying, "I'm civil" helps insulate you from any criticism that you are promoting injustice, that your choices are hurting others. Pointing to your good heart, your impeccable manners allow you to more readily deny that you have any role in making others suffer. You give to charity, you're a good father, you don't speed when you drive, you pay your taxes on time—you're civil. You wear the badge of civility to deny the fact that you turn a blind eye to mass incarceration; that you enthusiastically support political candidates who want to create harsher voting restrictions; that you want lower taxes, even if they devastate poor communities.

Civility is also remarkably effective at neutralizing opposition. Saying, "Be civil" to someone expressing legitimate political grievances transforms the conversation. Now the supposedly uncivil person must play by the terms or be chastised; they must prove that their demands are reasonable in the first place, that they aren't being extreme. They must spend their time proving that that they deserve to be taken seriously, rather than articulating their demands. The preacher of civility, however, having assumed the offensive position, leaves the conversation without having to defend their own position. This is how rulers maintain a society in which inequality is the norm and injustice an incontrovertible fact: they silence opposition by disqualifying its legitimacy from the start.

But these aren't the most dangerous uses of civility. Much more significant is the act of sanctioning forces of power such as the police, vigilante groups, racial terrorists, and prison wardens, who are deployed to discipline citizens labeled uncivil. Anytime you speak of civility, you're also speaking of incivility—people who break the law, who don't exhibit exemplary public etiquette, who aren't deferential to authority. Politicians, lobbyists, public intellectuals, and media elites determine what constitutes civil and uncivil behavior.

The meaning of these terms isn't set in stone. The troubling thing, however, is that these shifting definitions intersect with racism. Because we have long-standing racist myths in the United States that characterize black people as morally, culturally, and intellectually inferior to white people, their behavior is often treated with suspicion whether or not they are doing anything politically contentious. As they walk along the street, sit in a park, do their jobs, and, generally, live their private lives, they are assumed to be threatening, irresponsible, criminal, and dangerous.

Not everyone who talks about civility or incivility is a hardened racist. But once you have a society that traffics in these terms against the backdrop of racism, the language triggers authoritative actions: police are swiftly summoned to discipline undisciplined black youth; white citizens decide whether black people are legitimately enjoying public space; armed vigilantes determine whether black people live or die; and prisons get the final say for how long black people will be free. The link between racism and a politics of civility was formed long ago, and, so, this is how systemic racism persists with the participation of relatively few self-described racists.

We must remember this connection whenever we hear anyone talk about the need for greater civility in race relations. Keeping US history at the forefront of the argument illustrates that civility has never been neutral in its uses and impacts. Armed with this knowledge, progressives have a strong case for rejecting a politics driven by civility. It's not just that civility is regularly invoked to depress activism by saying what we can and can't do in the public sphere. It also empowers the criminal justice and prison systems to exacerbate pain for the black majority.

Although the history of civility in racial politics is bleak, we might still wonder whether the idea of civility is worth reviving in the fight for racial equality. Even if it has been used for nefarious ends, does it mean we should abandon it entirely? The more optimistic among us might wonder if we can modify civility, make it work for us, or use it in a strategic way for progressive ends.

The answers to these questions are decisive. Civility hasn't been the organizing principle of the most successful anti-racist thinkers and movements who have sought to dismantle US racism. They discovered, over and over again, that real political change happens through direct struggle, without obligation to decorum or propriety. Creating real political change requires us to confront unequal institutions rather than simply point out bad behavior. Shocking and provoking people—no matter how impolite the words or actions might seem—is necessary to wake the majority of people from their moral slumber. Disobeying unjust laws and taking disruptive action puts pressure on the levers of political, cultural, social, and economic power, and that pressure is what moves ruling elites to take notice and come to the negotiating table.

History shows us that successful leaders and movements name injustice and who is responsible for it without qualification or negotiation. It also shows that mobilizing allies who share our commitment to equality and freedom is infinitely more important than reaching across the aisle to try to make coalitions with people fundamentally hostile to our views. What's necessary is not following the rules of the game but instead constantly questioning whether the rules are just so that we can change how the game is played.

All of these tactics are part of an orientation I call "civic radicalism," which is the key to fighting racism. We can find this way of thinking and behaving in major anti-racist activists across US history: everyone from Frederick Douglass to David Walker, John Brown, and Harriet Tubman; from W. E. B. Du Bois and Ida B. Wells to Martin Luther King Jr., James Baldwin, Malcolm X, and Audre Lorde; and from the students of the Student Nonviolent Coordinating Committee (SNCC) to black feminists, labor activists, peace activists, and Black Lives Matter today.

All of these figures and movements turned away from civility when the stakes were highest. They knew civility had no role in the fight to gain freedom for the marginalized. Here's why civic radicalism is superior to civility as a political approach: A politics based in civility makes agreement among participants the prerequisite for political thought, whereas civic radicalism begins with the goal of liberation for all, regardless of who disagrees. Civility politics champion stability, but civic radicalism questions who counts in the public sphere and who doesn't, whose lives matter and whose don't. Civic radicalism unsettles what civility assumes has long been settled: the kind of community we are and want to be.

This broader goal, liberation, highlights why civic radicalism isn't the same thing as civil disobedience. Civil disobedience is a particular nonresistance tactic used by social movements to draw attention to unjust laws. So civic radicalism can and has often included instances of civil disobedience throughout history, but it's a broader and much more general attitude toward political engagement that involves the way we speak, think, organize, feel, and act. Direct action, too, is a source of civic radicalism's strength, but so, too, is a pragmatic assessment of what form it should take. The civic radical doesn't take up action for its own sake—just to do something—but thinks about the right conditions, the best alliances, and the specific institutions upon which to focus their activism.

Progressive citizens who care about racial and socioeconomic equality and who may identify as part of the Resistance might think that they are helping their cause when they talk about being civil, which means hearing both sides, reaching for compromise, and seeking consensus. But they are wrong. Knowing the story of civic radicalism shows why listening to both sides is a less effective strategy for justice than disruptive direct action; why greater empathy is less important than fiery criticism; why mass protests in the street are better than political organizations that file legal petitions or only want to engage Congress and sitting US presidents.

Achieving racial justice requires a revolutionary change in how we think. Whether we like it or not, civility isn't the answer. Political and socioeconomic elites who aren't affected by radical inequality are the greatest beneficiaries of civility. Their power—which is to say their enormous wealth, political influence, and unrivaled social status—isn't fundamentally tied to how civil they are. And yet, the most marginalized Americans are disproportionately asked, time and time again, to embody civility's noblest ideals. What they get in return when they take up the call to be civil is nothing but a pat on the back. But what they get when they don't obey the call to be civil is nothing they would ever want—police batons, jail time, the evisceration of a social safety net, and public shaming.

The task for any successful multiracial democratic movement is to fight oppression and, in doing so, to end discrimination against all people of color, to extend economic freedom to the poor, to give women equal dignity in society without the threat of sexual violence, and to allow LGBTQ citizens to imagine their identities in ways they see fit. Civic radicalism, not civility, is the way forward. To carry out the task of civic radicalism, we don't need a numerical majority but rather a committed minority willing to fight for what's right. In the inimitable words of James Baldwin,

> Majorities [have] nothing to do with numbers or with power, but with influence, with moral influence, and I want to suggest this: that the majority for which everyone is seeking which must reassess and release us from our past and deal with the present and create standards worthy of what a man may be—this majority is you. No one else can do it. The world is before you and you need not take it or leave it as it was when you came in.[5]

Chapter 2

CIVILITY DISTRACTS FROM INEQUALITY

In response to antislavery petitions sent by abolitionists on February 6, 1837, the distinguished senator from South Carolina, John C. Calhoun—who had been vice president first under the privileged scion John Quincy Adams in 1825 and then under the populist Andrew Jackson in 1829—valiantly took to the Senate floor to defend the virtue of slavery. Calhoun could have said any number of things to support this view: Might makes right. Slavery is a pragmatic way of keeping all interests happy. Natural rights don't exist and are the pipe dream of liberal idealists. But he didn't. Instead, he turned to what he saw as the lovelessness tearing the country apart:

> However sound the great body of the non-slaveholding States are at present, in the course of a few years they will be succeeded by those who will have been taught to hate the people and institutions of nearly one-half of this Union, with a hatred more deadly than one hostile nation ever entertained towards another . . . It is impossible under the deadly hatred which must spring up between the two great sections, if the present causes are permitted to operate unchecked, that we should continue under the same political system.[1]

Calhoun was described by contemporaries as having great political acumen. A Yale graduate and a trained lawyer, he knew that political power in the antebellum period was determined as much by who won a battle of ideas as it was by who controlled lawmaking, war, and the courts. Seizing the mantle of civility has always been a boon to the ruling elite. And so it was for slaveholders. Christianity was the bedrock of society, and politicians encouraged the public to imagine politics in moral terms as a way to cultivate popular support. Like countless proslavery politicians, Calhoun described the tension in American politics as a lovers' quarrel between a hostile, hateful North and a genteel South rather than acknowledging the moral abomination of trafficking human flesh. By framing the debate about slavery this way, he hoped to make Americans forget that there were 2.5 million enslaved people who made the cotton, sugar cane, tobacco, and coffee industries churn.

Civility is the perfect mask for defending a status quo that works well for elites but not so well for those they dispossess. Calhoun and other slaveholders worked hard to associate slavery in the public mind with the warm feelings toward civility that existed in the traditional Southern home and in the depths of Southerners' hearts. In doing so, he disconnected the idea of slavery from the idea of justice. In his hands, the argument about slavery became one that dismissed the promise of freedom for all in favor of an intense emotional attachment to and a twisted moral justification of the enslavement of millions of people.

The Virginia lawyer and small-time planter George C. Fitzhugh couldn't stop talking about slaveholders' civility in his *Cannibals All! Or, Slaves Without Masters* (1857), in which he said, "Slavery leaves but little of the world without the family," suggesting that because slaves were considered part of the family that owned them, they were spared the "selfishness" that occurs in human society outside the family structure.[2] Later, Fitzhugh, reiterates this inescapable loving bond between the slaveholder and the enslaved person, writing, "Love and veneration for the family is with us not only a principle, but probably a prejudice and a weakness."[3]

By focusing on the slavemaster's love, Fitzhugh whitewashed the "peculiar institution." He strove to keep from public consciousness the fact that the wealth of the nation depended on brutally extracted unpaid black labor, scarred black children, and raped black women. The master tends to his slaves, Fitzhugh contended, as a father shares life lessons with his children, when, in reality, a slaveholder is a self-interested business-man extracting free labor from his human property. The enslaved person is not, as Fitzhugh would have the public believe, a noble hardworking son in need of occasional discipline but rather a naked black person being whipped into submission with no repercussions from the law.

Proslavery forces upheld civility as a norm to which Northern abo-litionists needed to aspire. And uncivil black rebellion was something of which they were absolutely terrified. There was the ongoing Seminole rebellion that began in 1835, which saw Native Americans joining with escaped slaves to destroy twenty-one sugar plantations in Florida. During the *Amistad* Mutiny in 1839, fifty-three enslaved people killed the captain and cook on a schooner heading to Havana, Cuba.[4] The ever-increasing number of runaway plots and insurrectionary activities occurring in Georgia, South Carolina, North Carolina, Virginia, Louisiana, Alabama, Maryland, and Texas instilled great fear in the planter class.[5]

Calhoun endlessly invoked greater interracial compassion because he knew rebellion is what topples rulers from power. Whenever uncompro-mising resistance is on the rise, elites quickly redefine it as threatening to the common good, as a grave danger to decency and our ability to live peacefully together. Calhoun realized that the inalienable right of dem-ocratic revolution articulated in Thomas Jefferson's Declaration of Inde-pendence (1776) couldn't be safely restricted to white people. Nowhere was this clearer than in the failed rebellion plotted by an enslaved black-smith named Gabriel Prosser in Richmond, Virginia, in the fall of 1800, which was discovered before it could materialize. Upon hearing the news of Prosser's plan, Jefferson's friend James Callender warned in a letter to him that Prosser wanted "to massacre all the whites . . . and then march off to the mountains, with the plunder of the city . . . An idea truly worthy of an African heart!"[6]

Jefferson would, no doubt, have agreed with Callender's sentiment. Jefferson was instrumental in perpetuating the racist idea that is still invoked anytime we see a defiant black protest, expressions of black anger, or withering black social criticism against racial inequality: incivility is located in black biology—deep in the bones, heart, and blood. In *Notes on the State of Virginia* (1781), the Virginia slaveholder of Monticello, who personally felt slavery was abominable, had no qualms asserting that when danger is present, enslaved black Americans, while "at least as brave" as white people "have a want of forethought . . . They do not go through it with more coolness or steadiness than the whites."[7]

Discussions of black incivility paid rich dividends for slaveholders: the faults of enslaved people explained their enslavement. Nineteenth-century South Carolina writer William Gilmore Simms, whom Edgar Allan Poe flatteringly described as the greatest novelist the United States had produced, projected onto black people his own guilty conscience. "Slavish and superstitious," was how Simms described them, "anxious to luxuriate in forbidden pleasures; . . . envious of the wealth which they have not patience to wait for."[8] The enslaved were described as lazy so they could be more thoroughly exploited by the whip on the plantation, politically inept so they could be denied electorally, and excessive in their appetites so they could be given little to eat.

Defining black incivility in these ways was highly effective at helping proslavery forces avoid the question of what motivated such behavior. If they could convince the public that black people are just naturally criminal, then why would anyone look at laws and policies that inspire their righteous indignation or make them feel that resistance is worth dying for? Through deflection, they avoided the question of racial equality. After Gabriel Prosser's rebellion, for instance, the Virginia State House of Representatives turned to Jefferson, then vice president under John Adams, to raise funds for the Sierra Leone Company, the corporate body responsible for looking into black resettlement schemes that envisioned sending rebellious slaves from the US to the African continent.

Resettlement wasn't adopted; punishment was the answer. The state of Virginia publicly executed twenty-six black alleged coconspirators, including Gabriel Prosser, banned enslaved people from piloting boats, and barred lending enslaved people to others for hired work. Three decades later, Virginia used Nat Turner's rebellion—during which rebel slaves killed sixty white people in Southampton, Virginia, in 1831—as another opportunity to pass restrictive laws to undermine anti-racist resistance. These laws prohibited enslaved people from reading, disseminating printed materials, and congregating and preaching in public spaces. Virginia's new policy applied to free black and biracial citizens as well, and also targeted the white people who entertained the thought of assisting these groups in any of these activities. Why such a harsh response? A dear friend of Senator Calhoun, William Harper, in his *Memoir on Slavery* (1838) writes that if slavery is to exist, the master needs to retain the "power of punishment as will compel [slaves] to perform the duties of their station."[9]

Slaveholders weren't just paranoid. They were right to think that revolt emboldened free black and poor white citizens. Gabriel Prosser's refusal to be governed by unjust power, to live without complaint in decrepitude and bondage, could be contagious. No one knew this better than Jefferson. Years before Prosser's rebellion, when Jefferson had been living in Paris as the US ambassador to France, he heard the news about the Revolutionary War veteran Daniel Shays and his four thousand followers marching from western Massachusetts to overthrow the state government as a protest against economic injustice—specifically, high debt and excessive taxation. In a letter to William Stephens Smith, Jefferson explained why he thought Shays was a true democrat: Rebellion, he said, is integral to preserving liberty, sending a message to rulers that their people possess a "spirit of resistance . . . The tree of liberty must be refreshed from time to time with the blood of patriots and tyrants."[10]

These words were sacred to the most famous rebel of the nineteenth century, Frederick Douglass. After multiple unsuccessful attempts, this twenty-year-old black man escaped from slavery in Maryland on September 3, 1838, and headed north to New Bedford, Massachusetts. There, Douglass began building his reputation as a great antislavery activist and a towering American political thinker. Douglass's life illustrates that one person's civic radicalism can create a powerful terrain upon which to motivate people to progressive action. A big heart animated Douglass's interest in justice, equality, and democracy for all and led him to confront hierarchy—whether through word or public action but preferably through both.

In his booming prophetic voice, Douglass shared with thousands of people his descriptions of life before escape—his desire to read, his dreams of freedom, his love of poetry. In his rich baritone and with dramatic flair, he disproved Calhoun's view that slavery was uplifting. A decade after Douglass escaped, in 1847, he wrote a letter to his former slave master, Hugh Auld, in which he said, "Indeed I feel nothing but kindness for you all—I love you, but hate Slavery."[11] Douglass's loving feelings toward his former master didn't make him accept Auld's arbitrary power. He despised the institution of slavery, even if he could, remarkably, feel fond of those who made it go.

Douglass became a well-known orator under the tutelage of the most famous white abolitionist of the time, Massachusetts-based William Lloyd Garrison, publisher of *The Liberator* from 1831 to 1865 and founder in 1838 of the New England Non-Resistance Society. Eventually, Douglass left *The Liberator* and started his own newspaper, the *North Star*, in 1847, for which Garrison would never forgive him.

Douglass is now seen as bastion of civility, a black founding father who courageously spoke truth to power. But he didn't hold his tongue when he saw the self-interest behind polite words posing as goodwill. Before a packed audience of the Ladies Anti-Slavery Society in Rochester, New York, on July 5, 1852, in the speech "What to the Slave Is the Fourth of July?," Douglass denounced the perversion of the Declaration of Independence without mincing words. He scorned fake patriotism and American boasting about "your love of liberty" and "your superior civilization."[12] He castigated the poster child of bipartisan compromise—the US senator from Kentucky, one-time secretary of state, and slaveholder Henry Clay—as a "torturous and wily politician."[13] Douglass despised Clay's lifelong passionate support of the American Colonization Society, founded in 1816 by Presbyterian minister Robert Finley and supported by a string of presidents, including Jefferson, James Madison, Andrew Jackson, and Abraham Lincoln. Douglass called colonization "Satan."[14] He thought Garrison was right in his pamphlet, *Thoughts on African Colonization* (1832), when he said it was "agreeable to slaveholders" and loved by all those with "undying hostility to the people of color."[15]

In truth, Garrison himself had originally been in favor of black colonization but had rethought his position after listening to his allies among the black abolitionists in Boston, who didn't traffic in what was respectable. One of them, Maria W. Stewart, whose very presence as a woman in the public sphere scandalized misogynists, told an audience in February 1833 at the African Masonic Temple that it is necessary to fund public education and institutions of higher learning so black people could flourish in the US rather than be resettled abroad. Stewart followed the example of the Philadelphian known as the "gentleman of color," James Forten. Forten first thought an exploratory party to Africa might be good for black business, but upon learning that not one of the three thousand strong who showed up at a meeting at Mother Bethel Church supported it, he issued a condemnation of the idea in January 1817. Why should those who "were the first successful cultivators of America," he writes, "building this country with their blood, sweat and tears have no claim to enjoy and share in what they created?"[16]

As Stewart and Forten remind us, democracy is a battle over who belongs and why. But claiming belonging through words isn't enough. Direct action is necessary to change the world. Taking action is never easy, and it is easy to criticize the actions of certain individuals and groups in an unequal world. Every move is wrong, every decision unknown. What is necessary is acting with purpose and taking the heat afterward, knowing that all choices must be open to reevaluation.

Douglass questioned Garrison's commitment to the antislavery movement and eventually broke with his mentor, because he came to see Garrison's pacifism as a losing orientation, especially after Congress in 1850 passed the Fugitive Slave Act. This act permitted slave catchers to hunt fugitive slaves in Northern states such as Ohio, New York, and Massachusetts, for all intents and purposes, nationalizing slavery. As early as January 10, 1850, one observer recalled that, at the National Anti-Slavery Society convention, Douglass called for "armed resistance by blacks, declaring they possessed the right to kill to escape slavery."[17] Douglass knew first-hand what slaveholder authoritarianism looked like, having lived under the whip of his one-time master Edward Covey, as Douglass describes in his second autobiography, *My Bondage and My Freedom* (1855). Not long after being sent to Covey's plantation in January 1834, the sixteen-year-old Douglass had had enough. Covey, incensed by Douglass's brazenness, decided to tie his legs and flog him. But Douglass, gripped by a powerful force he couldn't fully articulate, wouldn't submit, even when Covey recruited the help of a fellow enslaved farmhand. In a physical struggle Douglass describes as lasting over two hours, he didn't back down, and, eventually, Covey simply gave up. His battle with Covey was "a turning point in my life as a slave," Douglass says. "It rekindled in my breast the smouldering embers of liberty . . . I was a changed being after that fight."[18]

From Douglass, we learn that physical resistance enlivens because it transforms the self. New possibilities for freedom—that one will not die, will not be demeaned—turn passive people into engaged citizens. Popular conceptions have it backward: activists don't just get involved; involvement creates activists. Think apolitical youngsters cutting class or violating curfew to experience the thrill of their first march, mothers and fathers standing against senseless gun violence, or teachers going on strike in states where striking is illegal.

But how we speak—verbal resistance—also raises the stakes about what matters. There is much to be gained from speaking in language that is impolite, uncompromising, direct, searing, unconditional, morally clear, and willing to challenge equivalences between good and evil. In his characteristic fiery rhetoric, Garrison was unafraid to tell his followers—by 1838 a staggering 250,000 of them—that they could accept no less than immediate emancipation for slaves. Even after his Non-Resistance Society disbanded in 1849, Garrison was clear in his assertion that "while a slave remains in his fetters, the land must have no rest."[19]

But Garrison matched his lofty words with action. He jeopardized his own financial gains and his personal safety by helping first Douglass and then other fugitive slaves who were part of the Underground Railroad, led by Harriet Tubman, whom Garrison referred to as "Moses." He wouldn't vote or hold political office on the basis of maintaining a certain ideological purity—his form of abolitionist protest. Narrowly escaping a lynching and seeing the Illinois editor Elijah Lovejoy meet that fate on November 7, 1837, Garrison remained steadfast in his view: "I deny the right of any people to *fight* for liberty," he said, "and so far am a Quaker in principle."[20]

Garrison's rejection of violent uprising explains, in part, why he was so affected by the text that had no peer in terms of its impact on the politics of the century: the novel *Uncle Tom's Cabin* (1852), written by the Maine-based white abolitionist Harriet Beecher Stowe. Within a year, it had sold three hundred thousand copies in the US and two million across the world. Stowe fictionalized for white Northern middle-class readers what Douglass vividly described in his autobiographies: black enslavement was horrific. When Douglass met Stowe in her home at Andover, Massachusetts, in February 1853, after noting that *Uncle Tom's Cabin* touched "the universal soul of humanity," he commended her "exalted sense of justice."[21]

But *Uncle Tom's Cabin* is no unqualified success. A simplified narrative that features the "triumph" of black civility ruins its emancipatory potential. The enslaved black man Tom, the novel's protagonist, is dying as a result of a vicious beating by Simon Legree, the slaveholder villain, and his overseers. Even on the verge of death, Tom expresses his hope for interracial reconciliation. "When we can love and pray over all and through all," he says, "the battle's past, and the victory's come,—glory be to God!"[22] Complex black lives should never be caricatured as the ground for white redemption, for cleansing white sins through unconditional forgiveness for every imaginable heinous deed. But this is exactly what Stowe tried to do.

Stowe wasn't alone in this endeavor. Arguably the greatest poet America produced in the nineteenth century, Walt Whitman, in his collection of poems and prose *Leaves of Grass* (1855), depicted black people as childlike innocents rather than autonomous human beings. Though Whitman was a critic of slavery, racial equality wasn't something he supported—as demonstrated through his membership in the Free Soil Party, formed in 1848 and incorporated into the Republican party by 1854, that conceived of an American West free of both slavery and black people, a frontier in which white laborers would finally be treated with dignity. It is no surprise after reading Whitman's work to learn that he came from a family of slaveholders and couldn't conceive of a true multiracial democracy. His memory of a black acquaintance from youth, "Old Mose," whom he describes as "very genial, correct, manly, and cute,"[23] could have been written by Stowe. And in his most famous poem, "Song of Myself," the runaway slave the poetic speaker encounters is described, upon arriving upon his doorstep, as "limpsey and weak," with "revolving eyes," and marked by "awkwardness."[24]

The decrees to "turn the other cheek" and "stand down," common during the antebellum era, demanded that enslaved people choose sides. When they were civil and compassionate toward their torturers, like Uncle Tom, then they were said to enjoy their lot, so there was no obligation to change it. But when they resisted crippling subjugation in whatever way they could, they were beaten and killed for their incivility. Even those who called themselves allies and understood the brutality of slavery scorned them. Nat Turner's rebellion, for instance, sent William Garrison into a fit of dismay bordering on panic. Violent resistance against a violent institution was not imagined by the white liberal as a necessary choice but rather as the first sign of an antiwhite race war. Notice how quickly a discussion of civility morphs into racism: Garrison confided in a letter to a friend that he was "horror-struck . . . What we have so long predicted,—at the peril of being stigmatized as an alarmist and declaimer, has commenced its fulfillment." Garrison was certain Turner's actions would lead to "a war of extermination."[25]

Reactionaries were emboldened by these rumors of a coming race war. The fantasy of unruly blackness was marshaled to counter talk of social transformation. Garrison's assessment was strikingly similar to that of Kentucky senator Henry Clay, who was a master at playing upon people's fears by constructing terrifying stories that had no basis in fact or history. Clay wrote to a friend in 1842 decrying abolitionists' insistence on immediate emancipation, which he feared would tear the Union apart. He argues that emancipation would necessitate white enslavement and that forcing states to free their slaves would cause a flurry of "blood, devastation, and conflagration"[26]

But Frederick Douglass could not be swayed by such racist fearmongering. He knew firsthand that enslaved people had good reason to fight. He insisted that Christian humanism was incompatible with slaveholder paternalism. His visit with Stowe inspired Douglass to write a novella, *The Heroic Slave* (1852), based upon the enslaved black revolutionary Madison Washington, who led a rebellion on a ship in 1841.

Douglass took up different identities—as a novelist, an orator, an editor, and a journalist—to get the job done. In this way, he was like one of his civic radical ancestors, the black abolitionist David Walker, who left his job writing for a leading abolitionist newspaper, *Freedom's Journal*, to pen and distribute the pamphlet *Appeal to the Coloured Citizens of the World* (1829). Walker moonlighted as a used-clothing salesman and was involved with the Boston Prince Hall Freemasons while living in the Beacon Hill neighborhood. Previously, in the 1820s, Walker had spent time with the African Methodist Episcopal Church (AME) in Charleston, South Carolina, around the time Denmark Vesey, a carpenter, community leader, and former slave, allegedly formed a conspiracy—which was later foiled—to burn the city of Charleston to the ground.[27]

Born free in Wilmington, North Carolina, in 1785, Walker died in 1830 on the front steps of his home—rumor spread that he was poisoned because he was a wanted man, but the likely cause was tuberculosis. His *Appeal* circulated widely by hand, especially in free black communities and even on some plantations. So threatening was it to slaveholders that they put a hefty $10,000 bounty on his head. In his *Appeal*, Walker said black freedmen who turned a blind eye to slavery were as complicit as—if not more than—white slaveholders in the suffering of enslaved people. "How we could be so *submissive* to a gang of men," he wondered, "whom we cannot tell whether they are *as good* as ourselves or not, I never could conceive."[28] Uncivil words instill anxiety in the powerful because they have a life of their own and can't die.

Walker's faith in resistance by any means necessary was like that of the white abolitionist Calvinist John Brown. Brown, with his piercing blue eyes and arresting gaze, was unafraid to call himself an anti-racist, no matter how shrill or loud he seemed to others. He accepted being called a "dyed in the wool" abolitionist as a compliment of the highest order. Fighting to the death for enslaved people and free black people—"his brothers and equals"—was, for him, a privilege.[29]

Because justice rather than civility was Brown's objective, he developed a reputation as a deranged terrorist, a misguided fanatic. But Brown wasn't crazy; he responded to the hand he was dealt. He arrived in Kansas in the fall of 1855 with his sons, after the Kansas-Nebraska Act of 1854 had allowed voters to decide the fate of slavery. The territory had a slave population of ninety thousand, and proslavery settlers were flocking to the territory in droves to skew the vote in favor of slavery.[30] The sitting president, the Northern Democrat Franklin Pierce, came out in support of the proslavery Kansas legislature and the Fugitive Slave Act, thereby rendering null and void the Missouri Compromise of 1820, which had prohibited slavery north of the Mason-Dixon Line.

Brown's staunch egalitarianism and sense of responsibility is a model of moral clarity. But his penchant for senseless violence is less admirable. On the night of May 24, 1856, in the town of Pottawatomie Creek, as proslavery "border ruffians" burned Kansas, Brown and four of his sons, equipped with rifles and knives, dragged five proslavery settlers—who didn't own slaves—out of their homes and notoriously hacked them to death. This gruesome act caused a public firestorm for its brutality. And even now, it requires condemnation, because it was motivated by vengeance rather than a desire for justice. No matter the intention or sense of righteousness, terror for its own sake is no foundation for freedom. What to Brown might have seemed a legitimate response, this kind of strike against an institution that enslaved, murdered, lynched, mutilated, and raped millions of people, then as now, is an unacceptable way to raise awareness about a cause. The larger question, then and now, is this: What can bring into existence a new egalitarian society in which all can thrive?

While Douglass defended the tactic of armed struggle against slavery, his pragmatism told him that Brown's mission to liberate the enslaved at a federal arsenal at Harpers Ferry, Virginia, would fail. In 1859, when

Brown invited him to join the raid, which is now seen as a major catalyst for the Civil War, Douglass declined. "Virginia would blow him and his hostages sky high," he said.[31] But Douglass viewed Brown as a friend and insisted that it was wrong to demonize one's allies, even if their tactics or timing were questionable. And so, Douglass didn't blame a mental disorder for Brown's actions, as others did. In an editorial entitled "Capt. John Brown, Not Insane," Douglass described him as a "glorious martyr of liberty" shortly after Brown was publicly hanged for treason for killing four at Harpers Ferry.[32]

Douglass wasn't the only one who idolized Brown, who was a hero in the eyes of the transcendentalist, naturalist, and essayist Henry David Thoreau, not for his indiscriminate killing but for his vision of equality. Thoreau's life is an example of how even loners, daydreamers, artists, and intellectuals who prefer their own company and the life of the mind over a social life can still do incredible work as civic radicals. Unlike Douglass's words, which he delivered to live audiences, Thoreau's were shrouded in mystery and couched in romantic allegories. But even someone who finds solace in the isolated woods of Walden Pond, where Thoreau lived from 1845 to 1847, in a small cabin owned by his friend Ralph Waldo Emerson, can leverage withering social critique for justice—through impassioned writing about consumerism, religious fanaticism, and political corruption.

That the introvert Thoreau eulogized John Brown in public—even though his community of Concord, Massachusetts, already perceived Thoreau himself as a pariah and his family begged him to stay quiet—speaks to what happens when fierce moral conscientiousness anchors our behavior. On October 30, 1859, Thoreau issued his statement at a Concord Church, where he called Brown a principled man "of rare common-sense" who didn't give in to "whim or transient impulse," but lived a purposeful life.[33] Thoreau himself lived according to his principles: He stopped paying his poll tax for four years to demonstrate his opposition to slavery and to the US annexation of Mexico. As a result, he spent one night in jail in July 1846. He helped to arrange safe travel farther north for fugitive slaves temporarily staying in his mother's Concord home.

Thoreau believed that a world all could enjoy would be a site of freedom and play, love and solidarity. In order to remake the world into such a place, he knew that we must eliminate the inequality that stands in the way of these things. He knew that abolishing racism isn't enough without ending imperialism, that abolishing slavery means little without ending extreme poverty. So when Thoreau announces at the outset in his now-classic 1849 essay "Resistance to Civil Government," "That government which governs best is what governs least," he isn't talking about what proponents of small government talk about in the twenty-first century. He isn't talking about doing away with high taxes or exposing a government conspiracy to intervene in people's private lives. What Thoreau is denouncing are the instruments of coercion upon which the state is founded and through which it enforces social inequality, namely the army and the police.

Thoreau was correct that maintaining civil order through the army and police demands unthinking patriotic obedience from the masses. The price of society's acceptance of such authority is that rich people, white people, and men get to enjoy their freedom, while women, nonwhite people, and poor people suffer under the enforcement of unjust laws. "Under the name of Order and Civil Government, we are all made at last to pay homage to and support our own meanness," Thoreau declares. "After the first blush of sin, comes its indifference; and from immoral it becomes, as it were, *un*moral, and not quite unnecessary to that life which we have made."[34]

Thoreau's uncivil politics of conscience is not uncontroversial. As with John Brown's actions in Kansas, we know that morality can morph into zealotry when the self-proclaimed righteous slaughter whomever stands in their way. In a pluralistic society, morality is subjective, so what happens when it is wielded by the wrong actor? Such a concern regarding individual actors is misleading, however, because it assumes that the backdrop for individual or even group violence is neutral. What we learn from Thoreau is that the conscientious people who may become violent— the ideologues, terrorists, demagogues, and fundamentalists—are less terrifying than the massive bureaucratic institutions that promote civility in the name of protecting our freedom but which also have ultimate authority to determine who lives and who dies—and by the millions.

Thoreau voluntarily risked his well-being by breaking the law and then bravely writing about being put into a steel cage and exposed to the soul death of the prison. In doing so, he laid bare the coercion upon which government is based. The choice couldn't have been clearer to him: Do we build a society of cages and fear, or one of freedom and hope? If we want to build a just society, it is paramount for us to place individual moral authority above the interest of national security, equality above realism, freedom for all above stability.

The greatest heroes are those ordinary people—the forgotten, the unknown, and the ignored—who take action under the radar rather than take to the podium. Everyday resistance may not always be memorialized, but it is what truly transforms the world. While Frederick Douglass was busy lecturing, a black woman by the name of Harriet Tubman was changing people's lives on the ground. Born into slavery in 1822 in Douglass's birth state of Maryland, Tubman escaped north in 1849, a decade after him, and became the leader of what would come to be known as the Underground Railroad. Its first stop was at the treacherous Southern plantations, and its last stop was in St. Catharines, Ontario, Canada. Tubman's deeds were louder than Douglass's words. She led; he persuaded. Her feet and hands were his voice and pen. Fearlessness and bone-deep religious conviction were her demeanor. Capacious hope and an ironclad sense of justice were her ideals. When asked what motivated her, Tubman replied, "Now I've been free . . . I know what a dreadful condition slavery is. I have seen hundreds of escaped slaves, but I never saw one who was willing to go back and be a slave."[35]

We often think of Tubman as a kindly freedom fighter, a conductor who just steered passengers along the railroad—the perfect subject for children's books. But she still matters for us because she was dead serious about her activism, and her terms were nonnegotiable. Douglass went north to escape, but Tubman made as many as nineteen return trips and, rumor had it, threatened to shoot anyone who complained about the journey. She broke laws she thought were unjust without seeking anyone's counsel. She repeatedly forged connections from scratch, collaborating with steamboat captains and railroad workers who could help her move fugitives more easily from place to place. No wonder John Brown asked her to join his raid on Harpers Ferry. She initially agreed but didn't make it because of failing health, in contrast to Douglass, who declined and felt guilt for many years afterward. Brown used the masculine pronoun *he* when speaking of Tubman. She was, in Brown's words, "the most of *man* naturally; that I *ever* met with."[36]

But Brown's compliment reflects a major problem we would be wise to remember: civic radicalism can be suffused with toxic masculinity. Heroism in the name of justice is seen by some activists as a man's game. But this ignores what is hiding in plain sight. Women throughout history have led and organized freedom movements and, even more significantly, questioned what emancipation means.

Sisters Angelina and Sarah Grimké left their cushy aristocratic lives in Charleston, South Carolina, to join a Quaker community in Philadelphia. Sarah became especially active in pushing for women's rights, while Angelina published her scorching antislavery tract addressed to fellow middle-class white women, *Appeal to the Christian Women of the Southern States* (1836), which demanded abolition, financial compensation for unpaid and stolen labor, equal legal rights, and education. Its publication unleashed a torrent of criticism. The South Carolina postmaster general burned copies of the pamphlet, police visited Angelina's mother's home, and Angelina's mother told her never to return. In 1838—after the sisters had already spoken to over forty thousand people on the lecture circuit—Angelina, with the help of three thousand abolitionists, pushed past a growing white mob blocking her entry to the hall in Philadelphia where an interracial audience had gathered to hear her lecture. After the event, white and black women interlocked hands to create a human barricade of sorts, barely escaping alive before the mob vandalized and burned the lecture hall to the ground. The next day Philadelphia newspapers described the abolitionists as the chief provocateurs, publicly displaying their impolite ideas in the face of decent men and women, who felt provoked and aggrieved.

Radical women abolitionists insisted that freedom was not one size fits all and that any freedom movement was incomplete without the inclusion of all voices. When Frederick Douglass first met the black radical abolitionist feminist Sojourner Truth in Northampton, Massachusetts, however, his desire to be civil blinded him from seeing her activism as an extension of his. He bristled at how Truth "cared very little for elegance of speech or refinement of manners."[37] His bitterness toward her may have had to do with the fact that her speech "Ain't I a Woman?," which she delivered in Akron, Ohio, on May 29, 1851, went further than any of the speeches he had written in its thinking about gender. For Truth, it was unacceptable that anyone would denigrate her either as a worker of strength equal to a man's or as a mother of many children. Douglass's reaction was, if anything, a sad reflection of masculine insecurity. Truth was following in the footsteps of Maria Stewart, who, in an address at Boston's Franklin Hall in 1832, had declared that rote domestic work did nothing but numb the mind and, so, needed to be replaced with education. "Washing windows, shaking carpets, brushing boots or tending upon gentlemen's tables," Stewart declared, "deadens the energies of the soul, and benumbs the faculties of the mind; the ideas become confined, the mind barren."[38] What Truth and Stewart said then is worth repeating now: racial equality is nothing without a revolution that results in women's freedom.

During the Civil War, civility again was used as an excuse to abandon racial equality. In a meeting with black leaders at the White House on August 14, 1862, the sitting president, Republican Abraham Lincoln, was quite emphatic in blaming the mere existence of black people in the United States for the war. Further, on December 31, 1862, the Great Emancipator, signed a contract with the notoriously unreliable entrepreneur Bernard Kock, agreeing to use federal funds to ship five thousand black people to Vache Island, next to Haiti, which Kock owned.

Douglass tried in vain to point out to Lincoln why he was wrong. Hidden beneath the polite way Lincoln spoke to black leaders, Douglass fumed, was a policy of ethnic cleansing. "It expresses merely the desire to get rid of them," he editorialized, "and reminds one of the politeness with which a man might try to bow out of his house some troublesome creditor or the witness of some old guilt."[39]

Such criticism fell on deaf ears, perhaps because Lincoln was obsessed with national stability rather than justice. Even before he became commander in chief, nothing bothered him more than lawbreakers. A twenty-eight-year-old little-known state representative in Springfield, Illinois, he was horrified to learn that a mob had taken the law into its own hands and burned to death a black man by the name of Francis McIntosh in St. Louis. But his horror was focused more on the lawlessness of the act than on the racist terrorism it illustrated. In his Lyceum address of January 27, 1838, Lincoln told his audience that even "bad laws . . . should be religiously observed."[40] Twenty years later, on February 27, 1860, Lincoln's focus on civility was again evident in his presidential campaign speech at Cooper Union in New York, in which he declared that John Brown was "no Republican" and his plot "absurd." Enslaved people showed their civility, he suggested, in their "affection for their masters and mistresses," implying that the enslaved were satisfied enough with their lives and therefore uninterested in fighting for freedom. Even in "all their ignorance," Lincoln said, slaves, more than anybody else, had believed Brown's insurrection would fail.[41]

Douglass first met Lincoln on August 10, 1863, and after that, his opinion of the president changed. He came to view Lincoln's public pragmatism as but a shield for personal sincerity, founded upon a respect for all, regardless of race. But at no point did Douglass use his increasing fondness for Lincoln as an excuse for accommodating ideas he knew were wrong. Even though the policy was unpopular and controversial, Douglass successfully pushed Lincoln to enlist black people in the Union Army and to advocate for the Thirteenth Amendment, which abolished slavery and was ratified in December of 1865.

Douglass did not hide his dissent or keep it private but instead made it visible to all. In this way, he unapologetically transformed the public square from one ruled by distrust and fear into one in which the democratic imagination could be explored boldly. Had Lincoln cast aside the example of Jefferson as statesman and slaveholder and instead led according to his idealism, his dream of downtrodden ordinary people sharing collective authority, refreshing the stale waters of the republic, he would have seen Douglass, who risked death to be free, as the finest extension of his legacy.

Lincoln never had the chance. When the bloody war ended on April 9, 1865, at Appomattox, Virginia, with Confederate Army commander Robert E. Lee's surrender and six hundred thousand dead, Lincoln had only six days to survey the aftermath before he was assassinated. A power vacuum emerged. Now the question for Douglass was not about resistance but about building a new American democracy for all.

Anytime there is political crisis, there is amazing potential to begin something new. Douglass knew this and so did the Republican Congress that he supported. But Southern Democrats knew this, too, and realizing Douglass's lifelong vision wasn't on their agenda. But Douglass continued to push for freedom. He led a delegation of thirteen men from the National Convention of Colored Men to Washington, DC, on February 7, 1866, to meet with Lincoln's successor, the Democratic president and rabid white supremacist Andrew Johnson. Douglass urged Johnson to endorse the right to vote for black men, but Johnson and his allies feared that the resulting social tensions would lead to a race war. Douglass argued that enfranchisement would have a transformative effect on American politics: "Let the negro once understand that he has an organic right to vote," he explained, "and he will raise up a party in the Southern States among the poor, who will rally with him. There is this conflict that you speak of between the wealthy slaveholder and the poor man."[42] Clearly Johnson was incensed by what he perceived as black impudence. As William Garrison had described Harriet Tubman, so President Johnson described himself as the "Moses" of ex-slaves. He told Douglass, "I have been their slave instead of their being mine."[43]

Almost immediately after assuming the office of the president, Johnson recruited civility to bolster inequality. Johnson was key in beginning what historian David Blight calls the "reconciliationist" narrative, which enabled Southern Democrats to dismantle Republican-initiated Reconstruction efforts. Talk of sectional reconciliation gave Johnson license to subvert the newly created Freedmen's Bureau, which he despised. He undermined the Bureau's efforts to help liberated black citizens build schools, receive medical care, start families, and get loans. Johnson pardoned ex-Confederates as long as they pledged an oath to the Union—a really good deal for them. He also fiercely opposed Radical Republican efforts to redistribute rebel-held land by the Bureau, which held roughly eight hundred thousand acres at the time. The utopian promise of forty acres and a mule went unfulfilled.

The aspiration of national civil reunion, of moving beyond historical animosity, is what provided cover for Southern states to circumvent the Thirteenth Amendment. As early as 1865, building off states' rights arguments, which Johnson wholeheartedly endorsed, many states instituted "Black Codes" that punished black people more severely than white people for committing vagrancy, violating labor contracts, and making crude gestures. Johnson's Republican successor, the general of the Union Army, Ulysses S. Grant, represented a distinction with no difference. Grant was no racist, but he was concerned not with redressing inequality but rather with maintaining market stability and the Republican Party's national influence. Reunion served these purposes well. When Grant first assumed power, in 1869, he forgot and forgave the sins of the Confederacy and acted as though slavery was a relic of the distant past. He said, "I shall have no policy of my own to interfere against the will of the people."[44] A decade after he left office, in his personal memoir, completed just before he died of cancer in 1885, he applauded the bravery and integrity of Robert E. Lee and didn't question "the sincerity of the great mass of those [Southerners] who were opposed to us."[45]

At every chance he got, Douglass reminded his countrymen that the Civil War was about slavery—period. Not about Southern culture, states' rights, or misguided honor. How we talk about the past matters, because it impacts how we understand the present. In his writing and his speeches, Douglass exposed the hidden power relations that diminished black freedom. He identified the conflicting interests at stake rather than exhorting the virtue of all sides of an argument.

But Douglass was no match for the elites who had their hearts set on the reconciliation between the key players in the shattered Union. The idea of reconciliation was especially suitable for the political class as a strategy to distract from the possibility of burgeoning multiracial democratic movements that existed after the war. Southerners were ecstatic when the newly elected Republican from Ohio, Rutherford B. Hayes, took office in 1877. Hayes rode to power on the promise of withdrawing all remaining federal troops from the South, thus putting an end to Reconstruction. Hayes promised working white people nothing, and the poll taxes slowly being instituted state by state as a prerequisite for voter registration disenfranchised as many of them as possible. And Northern industrialists—made uneasy by the rumblings of European socialism, especially the Paris Commune of 1871, and by the possibility after the Panic of 1873 that labor unionism would reach the American working class—were relieved when Hayes, only months after he took office, sent federal troops in to crush the Great Railroad Strike of 1877, which saw one hundred thousand workers in Maryland, Pennsylvania, and New York strike against steep wage cuts.

As these events unfolded, Douglass became a fixture of the Republican Party. As he aged, he sounded more like a pragmatist who knew the revolutionary change he once pined for might not be personally beneficial. What happens to civic radicalism once it finally gets a seat at the table? The results are mixed. Douglass didn't express full-fledged support for striking workers in 1877, and his ironclad faith in private property made him balk at redistributing Rebel-held land to emancipated black citizens after the Civil War, a position many Radical Republicans supported. But he did champion black access to loans and land when he became president of the Freedman's Savings and Trust Company in 1874.

Douglass believed strongly in equal rights for women, and he signed Elizabeth Cady Stanton's "Declaration of Sentiments" in 1848. But over time, he became convinced that activists could never win public backing for voting rights for both women and black people, and he decided to focus solely on winning the vote for black men. His decision led to a bitter falling out with Stanton. When she asked him to support a women's suffrage resolution at a New York State Senate meeting on January 23, 1867, Douglass didn't attend, and the resolution was easily voted down.[46] Three years later, black men won the vote when the Fifteenth Amendment was ratified in 1870

In the final analysis, Douglass was a revolutionary who couldn't stomach playing by the master's rules. Black politics, for him, was the exercise of unflinching irreverent prophetic critique, fearless direct action, and carefully finding friends and naming enemies. His words were erudite and his sentences perfectly constructed, but civility is not what Douglass, the ex-slave and rebel, counseled throughout his intellectual and public life.

Chapter 3

CIVIC RADICALS MAKE
DO WITH WHAT THEY HAVE

Seven months after Frederick Douglass died, on September 18, 1895, at the Atlanta Exposition Fair, the most famous living black American, the educator Booker T. Washington—known as the "Wizard of Tuskegee" after Tuskegee University, the historically black college in Alabama that he had established in 1881 and would preside over until he died in 1915— took the stage before a predominantly white crowd in Jim Crow Georgia. "To those of my race who depend on bettering their condition in a foreign land or who underestimate the importance of cultivating friendly relations with the Southern white man who is their next-door neighbor," Washington said, "[make] friends in every manly way of the people of all races by whom you are surrounded."[1]

From a leader who held immeasurable clout, Washington's words mattered greatly. Especially because, like Douglass before him, Washington was a man of firsts: the first black man to dine at the White House with Theodore Roosevelt, to whom he became the closest advisor on race; the first black man to have tea with Queen Victoria of England; the first black man to become the darling of super-rich white philanthropists John D. Rockefeller, Collis P. Huntington, and Jacob Henry Schiff.

Andrew Carnegie gave Tuskegee a massive gift of $150,000 to help build the university library. Above everything else, Washington was the first black man to be adored by many white Americans, because he was the polar opposite of Douglass. Washington was steadfast in his belief that racial progress depended on greater black humility. This meant a decisive turn away from the kind of political agitation Douglass had encouraged and modeled.

Douglass saw misuse of power, division, contestation, deceit, and hypocrisy everywhere he looked. But Washington saw the unachieved promise of racial reconciliation, forgiveness, generosity, and compromise. Indignation was the tone of Douglass's three autobiographies, struggle their message. Washington's tone was always conciliatory. He was born enslaved on a small farm in Virginia in 1856. In an article, he fondly remembered how, during Christmas in "Old Virginia," slaves joyously hung stockings on the mantel of their master's bedroom and in unison sang merry holiday songs.[2] At Hampton Normal and Agricultural Institute, Washington came under the tutelage of a white man, the former Union commander of a black regiment, General Samuel C. Armstrong, who became a second father of sorts. Washington arrived at the school to work as a janitor and then became a star student there.

When he opened the doors of Tuskegee University on July 4, 1881, Washington hoped he could encourage greater civility in a new generation of free black people and, as a Moses figure, lead them to the Promised Land. If only they could abandon the fiery rhetoric that Douglass had popularized, put their noses to the grindstone, and embrace what Tuskegee offered—an industrial education in the service of uplift, the opportunity to work silently and diligently at a trade—then they would be filled with self-esteem and be seen as worthy of respect from their white neighbors. Racial progress would result, eventually, gradually, with a growing class of black teachers, carpenters, artisans, and craftsmen. With the Republican betrayal of Reconstruction in 1877 and the return of Democratic rule in the South, Washington, the founder of what we now call black conservatism—whether out of principle, pragmatism, or both—came onto the scene preaching for racial reconciliation since, as he believed, slavery had long been abolished.

If Douglass had been alive to hear Washington's Atlanta speech, he would have been stunned. Washington may have been sincere in his conviction that civility was the answer, but, whether he liked it or not, he played right into the hands of the most vicious racists alive. These folks propagated the "Lost Cause" narrative, which held that the Civil War had been a battle to preserve Southern culture and states' rights, not slavery. And they fondly remembered what they imagined to be black civility on the plantation—the deference to oppressive rules, the moments of kindness to white planters, the compassion toward and care of white children. The point of this narrative was clear: enslavement hadn't been that bad. Maybe white domination and black subordination were exactly what black people, in their heart of hearts, preferred, or even secretly longed for.

For many white Southerners, black subjugation was the hidden meaning behind Washington's dream of racial reconciliation. "Uplift," if you were black, was a code word for knowing your place, of stepping down from whatever pedestal—no matter how small—you found yourself upon. As children, the white attendees at Washington's address had likely all read the *Atlanta Journal Constitution* editor Joel Chandler Harris's best-selling *Uncle Remus, His Songs and His Sayings* (1880). The enslaved main character, Uncle Remus—modeled on Harriet Beecher Stowe's character Uncle Tom—has only "pleasant memories of the discipline of slavery" as he retells the folk stories of Br'er Rabbit, Br'er Fox, and Br'er Bear to young children.[3]

The problem with these revisionist memories in the post-Reconstruction era wasn't just that they were patently inaccurate but also that they complemented what white racists believed to be the uncivil black menace unleashed by the abolition of slavery. In the racist mind, this nefarious monster called the "New Negro" was emboldened by greater voting rights, newfound economic independence, and a slightly improved social status. Senator James K. Vardaman, who had served as an army major during the Spanish-American War and who was known as the

"Great White Chief," wore the term "redneck" with pride and celebrated the fact that his state, Mississippi, had the highest number of lynchings in the 1890s. He despised "spoiled" black farmhands, sharecroppers, and tenants—who made up 75 percent of the farmers in his state. In the same breath, he longingly remembered his faithful black "mammy" who looked out for him with the "tender care of a mother."[4] Similarly, the best-selling author of children's books and short stories Thomas Nelson Page, who served as ambassador to Italy under President Woodrow Wilson during the First World War, described antebellum plantation life as rife with "warm friendship and tender sympathy." But looking at freedmen at the turn of the century, Page saw people who were "lazy, thriftless, intemperate, insolent, dishonest, and without the most rudimentary elements of morality."[5]

Controlling this imagined specter of black incivility became one primary reason for racists to set out on a campaign that devastated black America. Its name was white supremacy; its law was Jim Crow. The cornerstone of Jim Crow was the US Supreme Court case *Plessy v. Ferguson* (1896), which declared de jure what had been swiftly becoming a de facto reality. Racial segregation was constitutional, the justices said, because the separation of white and black people at public fountains, in schools, on trains, and in restaurants could still be equal. Additionally, Southern states introduced poll taxes, literacy tests, and grandfather clauses, causing black civic participation, robust before Jim Crow—voting rates were as high as 90 percent among black voters in many areas during Reconstruction—to plummet. In 1896 Louisiana, there were 130,000 black voters. But by 1904, the number had fallen to 1,342. In 1906 Alabama, 3,654 black men, as opposed to 205,278 white men, were registered to vote.[6]

When citizens are dominated, esteemed public intellectuals are usually the ones supplying the arguments. Take the idea that voters need to take responsibility for making better choices and, generally, be upstanding citizens rather than complain about bad politicians. It was pioneered for racist ends a century ago. Among the most notorious was the work of the distinguished historian William A. Dunning of Columbia University. In a 1901 essay for the widely read *Atlantic Monthly* magazine,

Dunning proclaimed that Reconstruction had failed because of black ineptitude at political leadership. Positioning black people as uncivil villains who engaged in "vicious" "tricks and knavery" gave his readers an excuse to feel sympathy for white Democrats and Klansmen. According to Dunning, since black people were thieving, lying, cheating, and stealing, then the real freedom fighters, the white redeemers who were hard at work restoring order in former rebel states, needed to be championed.[7]

Racial terrorists wholeheartedly embraced this thinking. Organized white farmers in the South, known as "whitecaps," burned black farms to the ground and executed anyone who dared to protest. They did these things in broad daylight, without any shame or fear of legal repercussion. Some all-white Southern municipalities became known as "sundown towns," in which black presence during the day was barely tolerated but after dark was illegal and thus treated as an invitation for target practice.

Blurred, too, was the line between extralegal and legal servitude. The Thirteenth Amendment of 1865 abolished chattel slavery and involuntary servitude except as a punishment for a crime. In some counties in which black incarceration had been just 1 percent that rate jumped to 90 percent by the 1870s. Almost immediately after the Thirteenth Amendment was ratified, the convict lease system emerged, creating a condition in which those convicted for petty crimes such as vagrancy would be forced to work for private companies for no pay. Over time, this arrangement became the chain gang—prisoners put to work for public services. Taking advantage of free prisoner labor was characterized by elected officials as a way to keep government slim and efficient. But in truth, it was neo-slavery with the patina of progress.

Armed white militias, who trained their wrath on free and prospering black communities, rose during Reconstruction, becoming an epidemic of staggering proportions by the end of the 1890s. They deputized themselves as police officers whose purpose was to quell presumed black disturbance, to preserve civil peace. Nowhere were they more brazen than in the 1898 coup in Wilmington, North Carolina, during which a white gang of two thousand overthrew the democratically elected city government and massacred dozens of black residents. For one of the white militia's leaders, the former Democratic congressman and eventual mayor of Wilmington, Alfred Waddell, it made perfect sense to describe the event as a "race riot"—the first time this term was used—because the existence in the town of black businesses, elected officials, and a vibrant black press, the *Wilmington Daily Record*, was a direct threat to white political power.

Not surprisingly, Waddell placed the blame for the riot upon the shoulders of black leaders who failed to answer his ultimatum to leave the city or be forcibly removed. "The old government had become satisfied of their inefficiency and utterly helpless imbecility, and believed if they did not resign they would be run out of town," he told the press later. "I believe the negroes are as much rejoiced as the white people that order has been evolved out of chaos."[8] The man who would become North Carolina's governor several years later, Charles B. Aycock, went further, defending the white freedom fighters as upstanding, decent men, part of the middle class. "This was not an act of rowdy or lawless men," he said. "It was the act of merchants, of manufacturers, of railroad men—an act in which every man worthy of the name joined."[9]

Two weeks later, in Washington, DC, a spontaneous meeting was convened by the most influential black journalist of the time, T. Thomas Fortune, a civic radical who had founded the militant National Afro-American League in 1887. Fortune spoke for most of the members of the delegation when he denounced President William McKinley's assertion that, despite pleas from black activists to send federal troops to Wilmington to quell the uprising, McKinley had no constitutional authority to do so because the sovereign state of North Carolina hadn't requested federal assistance. This wasn't surprising. After all, McKinley, like a string of presidents before him, had assumed office with a plea for national reunion, which was a coded term for states' rights. In his inaugural address of 1897, he proclaimed, "The North and the South no longer divide on the old lines."[10]

In his decidedly uncivil DC speech, Fortune went on the offensive, blatantly accusing McKinley, whom he had once campaigned for, of "glorifying rebellion, mobocracy, and the murder of women and children."[11] Fortune's speech reminds us that no authority figure, regardless of position, is beyond the reaches of withering critique. This civic radical's indictment of the sitting president of the United States highlights the fact that the willful inaction and utter neglect of a leader can be as harmful as criminal action.

Fortune's blistering words were in lockstep with the Afro-American League's founding message of resistance, conceived at the annual dinner of the Charles Sumner Union League in Hartford, Connecticut, in January 1884. It was there that Fortune called for black leaders to "Agitate! . . . Until the protest shall wake the nation from its indifference."[12] Booker T. Washington, who was not yet a well-known figure on the national stage preaching racial reconciliation, heard this credo and, in a letter to Fortune, expressed his exhilaration about the potential to "push the battle to the gate."[13] Fortune developed a close personal friendship with Washington, his fellow Southerner, and ghostwrote articles for him, for which he was paid a nominal fee. As Washington became a renowned public figure, Fortune's zealous editorials elevating him as a Moses figure tarnished Fortune's reputation among his revolutionary peers, but this writing was a source of financial support that kept his newspaper, the *New York Age*, solvent. Continued distribution of his paper was the way Fortune thought he could best make a public impact.

No doubt, strategic alliances between movements struggling to liberate the oppressed have always been the lifeblood of civic radicalism. But not if these alliances squash the revolutionary spirit. Deep down inside, Fortune must have known that the quest for advancement within political institutions, which aim to transform dissent into polite disagreement, is futile for political agitators. Most likely because of his reputation as a civic radical, Fortune was unceremoniously passed over when he sought the appointment as head of the Afro-American Literary Bureau under McKinley, and he also failed to win the ambassadorship to Haiti he so desperately wanted during Teddy Roosevelt's presidency.

On the level of collective action, when all was said and done, Fortune never moved Washington to change his tune about the necessity of black political withdrawal. But Fortune was no accommodationist. In private letters to Washington, he wrote about Roosevelt with derision. He saw the affable president as nothing more than an imperialist who preached jingoism in Cuba and the Philippines. And, ultimately, Fortune said, the president was an opportunist who cared about progressive politics only as long as they were cleanly severed from anti-racism.

Throughout Fortune's long life, his political thought remained decidedly opposed to Washington's. A graduate of Howard University and a trained lawyer, Fortune, a native Floridian—who had been born a slave in 1856—had seen firsthand the confluence of political corruption and violence during Reconstruction: Politicians were stuffing their pockets with kickbacks, and the Klan was so active that Fortune's father, Emanuel, who was elected one of the only black delegates to the Florida senate in 1868, carried a loaded gun at night on his way home. Fearing the worst, Emanuel prepared methodically detailed plans for his children in case he was executed.

Such a climate of absolute fear, coupled with the ever-present threat of incarceration and early death, would have encouraged even the most resilient citizens to learn how to become invisible—unseen and unheard. But Fortune did the opposite. He first made his name at the *People's Advocate* in Washington, DC, in 1876, before becoming the editor for the short-lived *Globe* newspaper, which then became the *New York Age*. Called the "crank of the colored press" by his friend Calvin Chase, Fortune wanted to reveal the forces working to suppress the expanding black voter base, forces wielded by people terrified of black political power. In 1883, parts of the Ku Klux Klan Act of 1871 were declared unconstitutional, which meant that the US president was no longer able to effectively target white supremacy organizations like the Klan. The Supreme Court, in an 8–1 decision, also declared the public accommodation clause of the Civil Rights Act of 1875 unconstitutional, which removed protections against racial discrimination in public transportation and in jury selection and service. In response to these reactionary developments, Fortune put it bluntly: "There is no law in the United States for the Negro."[14]

Washington dreamt of black entrepreneurialism, but inequality was at the forefront of Fortune's mind. In Georgia, a train conductor shuttled all black passengers to the smoking car, in spite of the fact that some of them had paid more for seats in the regular cars. When a judge ruled that it was the conductor's right to do so, Fortune promised to "kick down any fellow who attempts to enforce such robbery."[15] During the railroad strike of 1886, he excoriated newspapers that urged black workers to cross the picket line for personal betterment, writing, "The black man who arrays himself on the side of capitalism as against labor would be like the black man before the war taking sides with the pro-slavery as against the anti-slavery advocates."[16]

Had Washington truly considered Fortune's perspective, he would have seen why the Negro Business League of which he was so proud, which saw anywhere from five thousand to forty thousand members worldwide and which boosted black entrepreneurs, landowners, and professionals through its motto of "Buy black," would do little for black workers. In 1907, in Georgia, Alabama, and Mississippi, about one out of three black workers were indentured servants. During the Jim Crow era, it was not uncommon for residents of these states to hear bloodhounds barking in the countryside or to see these dogs with their handlers searching for fugitives fleeing debt slavery, known as "peonage."

Black sharecroppers were trapped in impossible poverty: They couldn't escape the escalating debt they had accrued through massive interest rates on their rent—25 percent or more. If a tenant wanted to move, the debts would remain; if they wanted to do business with someone else, the law forbade them from doing so. If they had a bad yield of a crop in any given year, they would still owe their landlord money they simply didn't have—and if they couldn't pay, they were forced to take out more loans and work harder.

In Fortune's magnum opus, *Black and White: Land, Labor and Politics in the South* (1884), written with an eye toward swaying public opinion, he convincingly showed that Jim Crow authoritarianism protected the unequal distribution of wealth and the vested class interests in the United States. He eviscerated the position held by the social Darwinist and Yale University sociologist William Graham Sumner, who brought Herbert Spencer's "survival of the fittest" doctrine to US economics. This was during the Gilded Age, when profits boomed for robber barons like Vanderbilt, Carnegie, and Rockefeller and life was miserable for just about everyone else.

Sumner believed that these captains of industry should rule and that their reign would be characterized by gentility and benevolence. But in his book *What Social Classes Owe Each Other* (1883), there is a close connection between Sumner's argument that "poverty is the best policy," and his view that some "races have degenerated and settled into permanent barbarism."[17] Once government is seen as having as its sole objective the protection of individual rights, then it will do nothing to deal with economic and social inequality. "I know it is not fashionable for writers on economic questions to tell the truth, but the truth should be told, though it kill,"[18] Fortune writes at the conclusion of *Black and White*. His thesis was this: "Poverty and misfortune make no invidious distinctions of 'race, color, or previous condition.'"[19]

Radical arguments matter for changing the conversation, but public engagement is how you expose a society in which lies are passed off as truth and civility demands inequality. Fortune tried to live his politics. After he was denied a drink at a bar in the Trainor Hotel on Thirty-Third Street in New York in June 1890, he stood his ground, before the owner asked another patron to forcibly push him out, with the aid of a cop. Fortune was charged with disorderly conduct and held in jail for three hours without being able to call a lawyer. The following day his case was dismissed, but not before word had spread uptown to Harlem and Fortune became known as a great example of everyday resistance. A fund, made up of private donations, was soon set up to assist Fortune in his civil rights lawsuit against the Trainor Hotel. With the representation of the African American attorney T. McCants Stewart, Fortune received one thousand dollars in compensation from an all-white jury.

But Fortune's confrontational style was never Washington's tactic. So as not to ruffle any feathers, after a white mob burned and looted black Atlanta businesses and murdered black citizens in September 1906, Washington issued an editorial calling for "patience."[20] When a mob of five thousand did the same in Springfield, Illinois, in August 1908, he kept quiet. That same year, as his train was passing through Lula,

Mississippi, Washington could see in the distance two lifeless black bodies, hanging from the branches of trees. But even then he continued to minimize the problem. This was not a national issue, but a local one, he commented in a letter to a friend, one of the problems "that so frequently occur in that state."[21]

It's true that Washington did, at times, condemn racial violence, as he did in a famous op-ed that appeared on February 29, 1904, in the *Birmingham Age-Herald*. But in the same article he failed to challenge the lie of black sexual deviance upon which lynching was founded: "Within the last fortnight three members of my race have been burned at the stake . . . Not one of the three was charged with any crime even remotely connected with the abuse of a white woman."[22] Washington went even further in a 1906 speech to a largely white audience at Vanderbilt University in Tennessee, placing blame on black women who dared to have intimate relationships with white men. "It is not always easy for us to make such a woman feel the weight of our condemnation," he said, "when in too many cases she is supported in ease, sometimes in luxury, by members of your race."[23]

Washington was clearly not a civic radical; civic radicals never hide their anti-racism while publicly projecting an apolitical image to the ruling elite. For example, Washington quietly funded voting rights litigation, including the suit brought by the Afro-American Council, which in 1899 challenged the constitutionality of Louisiana's grandfather clause exempting poor whites from voting restrictions placed on black people. But when a black man by the name of Tom Harris, having barely escaped a throng of white vigilantes intent on murdering him, came to Washington's home in the dead of night in need of medical attention, the Wizard would not let him in. Instead, Washington hid Harris away off campus before arranging transport to Montgomery, Alabama. Washington never admitted that he had helped Harris—even after black editors such as John Mitchell Jr., of the *Richmond Planet*, excoriated him for callously turning away a wounded man—because above all he wanted to burnish his apolitical public image. Without this correction, white supremacists were able to maintain the myth that not even black people would stand in the way of vigilante terror.[24]

While he helped to train a generation of black professionals at Tus-kegee, Washington worked at least as hard to preserve his own clout and spread his conservative platform. He had a hand in everything from de-termining the content of black newspaper editorials to obtaining grants for black colleges; from securing prized venues and economic support for black musicians and artists to directing the kind of research black professors would undertake; from recommending political appointees in the judicial system to offering names of nominees for federal agents. Washington was unwilling or unable to tolerate dissent. If things didn't work out to his liking, he unleashed his secret police, an army of spies in the world of black education, journalism, and political activism, among whom Melvin J. Chisum was the most active. Chisum, a one-time field secretary for the National Negro Press Association, acquired confidential information, threatened extortion, and spread false information against all whom Washington deemed too militant and radical.

Southern racists despised Tuskegee's goal of educating black people, which is still the brightest spot of his legacy. But many racists adored him for preaching black civility. One such figure, the North Carolina native and writer Thomas Dixon Jr., claimed to have "the greatest admiration" for Washington. In 1906, he offered Washington $10,000 to publicly de-nounce the aspiration for black social equality. Washington was indig-nant—he didn't even respond. And Dixon was likely baiting him.[25]

But Washington's message of black withdrawal from the political sphere resonated with Dixon. A first-rate opportunist, Dixon first turned to politics because he was a failed actor and then turned to writing be-cause he was a failed preacher. His best-selling melodramatic novel *The Leopard's Spots* (1902) features depthless characters in a punchless plot that spools out one banality after another. But perhaps this kind of acces-sibility is what made his book influential. It inspired D. W. Griffith's film *The Birth of a Nation* (1915), in which members of the Klan are character-ized as heroic as they lynch a black Civil War veteran. In the movie's final scenes, these KKK members ride on horseback to rescue a white woman from marrying another black Civil War veteran. The sitting president, Woodrow Wilson, screened the film at the White House and praised it effusively and unequivocally. This attention was crucial in spurring the KKK renaissance in the 1920s, when membership peaked. In August 1925, twenty-five thousand members marched in Washington, DC.

Dixon's work is a reminder that white supremacist violence is often a sign of weakness, rather than strength; its aim is to stitch up internal community disagreements, to attempt to make what is broken whole. In *The Leopard's Spots*, the naïve white man, Charles Gaston, insists that lynching is a "sin" and that he has "no hatred" for black Americans, but when the child of a one-legged Confederate veteran goes missing, Gaston and the crowd know exactly who is to blame. Dixon writes, "In a moment the white race had fused into a homogeneous mass of love, sympathy, hate and revenge. The rich and the poor, the learned and the ignorant, the banker and the blacksmith, the great and the small, they were all one now. The sorrow of that old one-legged soldier was the sorrow of all; every heart beat with his, and his life was their life, and his child their child."[26]

To understand why a certain form of civic love can be so troubling—if it is narrowly directed toward only those of one's own race—we need only look at photos of lynchings (from 1880 to 1968, 3,446 black people) and notice the hundreds if not thousands of white people in the crowds—men, women, often children—smiling, laughing, and waving as mutilated bodies hang above them. The terrifying thing is that lynchers believed that their terrorism was about preserving the peace and upholding the sacred honor of family—the most common explanation for this heinous crime was the patently false idea that black men were sexually assaulting white women. Love of white people for each other was used as an excuse to murder and intimidate scores of black people.

Dixon was but a popular entertainer, while Democratic US senator "Pitchfork" Ben Tillman from South Carolina was a politician with power to make policy. Tillman was too young to fight for the Confederacy but old enough to partake in Reconstruction-era violence. At age thirty, he enthusiastically became a Red Shirt, a member of a white paramilitary "rifle club" that received notoriety in 1876, after Tillman led an attack on an all-black regiment organized by the state's Republican governor and took part in the murder of six black freedmen in what became known as the Hamburg Massacre.[27]

Tillman, who fondly recalled this grisly event throughout his life, thought white supremacy was not a shameful term but rather a badge of honor. So he took to the Senate floor on January 21, 1907, to redefine the true victims of the fallout from the Civil War. They weren't white women, and they certainly weren't black men. The real victims were the lynchers themselves. Any percolating talk of federal antilynching legislation was an insult, Tillman insisted. In fact, the crux of Tillman's speech was a push for legislation to deny black Americans their Fourteenth Amendment right to citizenship. Tillman characterized racial violence as the natural extension of "unwritten laws," a necessary solution to a painfully slow legal system: "When stern and sad-faced white men put to death a creature in human form who has deflowered a white woman, . . . they have avenged the greatest wrong, the blackest crime in all the category of crimes . . . They are looking to the protection of their own loved ones."[28]

One view that we might hear today is that enlightenment is the antidote to racism—if only hardened racists would read good history and literature by people of color and realize that all people are part of one human family! But lynchers do not and never did care about facts. To Tillman and his allies, nothing was more precious than rejuvenating the manhood lost through Gilded Age economic inequality and changing norms about the family.

Empathy is one major response to domestic terrorists like white mass shooters today: Are they mentally ill? Have they suffered recent or long-term hardship, such as being laid off? What were the motives that made them resort to such heinous acts? White progressives asked the same questions over a hundred years ago. For example, Jane Addams, the Chicago-based feminist and founder of the social service organization Hull House, denounced lynching but tried to understand the motivations of the men who "honestly believe that this is the only successful method of dealing with . . . crimes" and "who say that most of these hideous and terrorizing acts have been committed in the name of chivalry, in order to make the lives and honor of women safe."[29] Harvard University psychologist and professor William James, in a 1903 letter to the editor of *The Republican*, was repulsed by "a lynching epidemic" that could only be stopped if the mobs' "leading citizens" were hanged. Yet James excused the participating white masses, who were pawns, "average men, victims of the moment when the greatest atrocities are committed, of nothing but irresponsible mob contagion."[30]

This was the progressive message: Violent means are abominable, but who can *really* say what racists *really* feel, or that—in their heart of hearts—their cause isn't grounded in a distorted sense of justice? The problem here is that when progressives focus on the motivation of perpetrators of violence, before we know it, our attention is on the pain of the perpetrators rather than on the people whom they terrorize and destroy.

Psychoanalyzing terrorists is not the answer to terrorism. No one knew this better than a black feminist Thomas Fortune greatly admired, Ida B. Wells. After seeing black businessmen Will Stewart, Calvin Mc-Dowell, and her friend Tommie Moss lynched for opening a grocery store in Memphis, Tennessee, that competed with a white man's nearby store, Wells—using the pseudonym "Iola"—minced no words in her March 2, 1892, pamphlet *Southern Horrors: Lynch Law in All Its Phases*. Her meticulous research detailed how the imagined black sexual predator was only the most sensational justification for lynching. She found that white mobs lynched for just about any reason—vagrancy, supposed threats, being in the wrong place at the wrong time, looking in the wrong direction, or, sometimes, for no specific reason at all.

Through firsthand interviews, Wells was able to successfully debunk the myth of black male hypersexuality. She showed how many interracial relationships involving black men and white women were in fact consensual, and even initiated by white women. Lynching, she came to understand, wasn't about chivalry but had a clear social function: it swiftly effaced expanding black electoral possibilities in the post-Emancipation era. "Men who stand . . . for devotion to the principles of equality and justice to all," she writes, referring to Christians and journalists, among others, "do not see that by their tacit encouragement, their silent acquiescence, the black shadow of lawlessness in the form of lynch law is spreading its wings over the whole country."[31]

Wells's example is a model for our time. She illustrates the difference between rigorous analysis and impartiality. A desire for impartiality brings lies and misconceptions into the conversation in the name of objectivity. No equivalence is possible between the acts of the racist white nationalist, who believes people of color are inferior and behaves accordingly, and the acts of the anti-racist, who knows the racist is wrong and does everything to stop him. Events are not "racially charged" or filled with "racial tension"; they are racist. Euphemisms such as these are choices—and distortions of fact.

Southern Horrors was widely read, and as a result, Wells became well known—and a target. The pamphlet was too much for whites who couldn't stomach a black woman questioning their version of events. A "brave woman" was what the elder statesman, the seventy-four-year-old Douglass, just before his death, called Wells in his preface to *Southern Horrors*.[32] Racists soon destroyed the offices of the *Free Speech* in Memphis where Wells was housed, while she was on a trip up north. Such costs are to be expected, but the civic radical transforms constraint into opportunity. As the *Free Speech* was burning, Fortune met Wells in New Jersey. He told her never to go back to Memphis and helped secure speaking engagements for her, while giving her a platform at his *New York Age*.

Fortune convinced Wells she was worth more alive than dead as a martyr; her talents could be better used for rallying public opinion in her antilynching crusade. So Wells sailed across the Atlantic in 1893, and again in 1894, and stirred the British masses in ways that were unprecedented.[33] Few were as instrumental as Wells in proving the political power of black feminism and laying bare the intersection between racism and patriarchy.

From the time she was a child born into slavery in 1862 in Holly Springs, Mississippi, Wells would never ever back down or be domesticated. In an era when respectability was the name of the game, Wells was a throwback to the old-school radical abolitionism of Harriet Tubman. Her dedication to justice was staggering. On September 15, 1883, the twenty-year-old was traveling by train from Memphis to her rural teaching post in Woodstock, Tennessee, when she was told by a racist conductor that she couldn't sit in the first-class section—a section in which she had sat during many previous trips. Wells objected to the conductor's demand that she sit in the smoker car, which was filled with choking fumes due to its placement right next to the engine. After Wells was forcibly dragged out of the first-class car kicking and screaming—while many white passengers applauded the conductor's efforts—she claimed she would rather get off the train than follow the conductor's orders. She returned to Memphis, where she petitioned a lawsuit, using a then-existing Tennessee law that demanded equal public accommodation for black and white citizens. A Memphis circuit court decided in Wells's favor, awarding her five hundred dollars' compensation.[34] Several years later, in 1891, Wells was fired from her teaching post in the Memphis public school system because she wrote an editorial denouncing the lack of resources in segregated black schools and the sexual harassment of black women teachers by the education board's white members.

Wells would eventually settle in Chicago in 1893. After initially arriving there to protest the exclusion of black Americans from the various exhibits at the World's Columbian Exposition—a world's fair held in honor of the four-hundredth anniversary of Christopher Columbus's arrival on US shores and to showcase the fruits of American capitalism and culture—she was struck by the city's vibrant black community. Between her arrival in Chicago and the year 1930, when she became one of the first black women to run for elected office in her bid for the Illinois state legislature, Wells revived the militant National Equal Rights League. Among other things, the League fought against bills prohibiting interracial marriage in Washington, DC, and against congressional legislation in the late 1910s that sought to ban or place stringent quotas on African migration to the US. Wells organized hundreds of Chicago's black women voters, whom she registered through the Alpha Suffrage Club, which she cofounded in 1913.

Wells gave material assistance and logistical support to newly arrived black Chicagoans escaping from the South by creating the Negro

Fellowship League (NFL) in 1910. As a community center equipped with a reading room, refreshments, a gaming area, job placement services, and weekly lectures, the NFL offered a safe haven for black citizens who, because of racism, were excluded from organizations like the Chicago Young Men's Christian Association (YMCA). Wells's mentorship continued when, as the first black woman probation officer for the Chicago juvenile court, she was responsible for eighty-five young people. Wells took this position not only to help fund the NFL but also to take the power away from the apathetic or racist probation officers who were tasked with policing Chicago's black youth.

As Ida Wells so elegantly illustrates, civic radicals make do with what they have: if the public sphere is policed, they turn to the editorial pages to stir conscience; if the franchise is restricted, they politicize the community; if their voice is delegitimized, they speak anyway, louder; if their identity is denigrated, they turn the tables on those who denigrate it. Personal experiences have a way of upping the ante for civic radicals and changing what a life in struggle means.

This reasoning inspired a student of Harvard psychology professor William James's who became a Harvard-trained sociologist and built a career that was the antithesis of Booker T. Washington's: W. E. B. Du Bois. As a black man born in 1868 in Great Barrington, Massachusetts—a majority white town with a small free black population—Du Bois was threatened by racial violence in a way that James could never be, since he could rail against it from the security and privacy of both white privilege and the ivory tower. Du Bois grew up going to integrated public schools and was encouraged by some of his white teachers to pursue the life of the mind. But deep down inside, he knew his freedom and even their respect for his humanity were often dependent upon their whims. This is why Du Bois neither excused the violence of whites nor characterized it as a spontaneous collective emotion. It was about intimidating black people, pure and simple, so that they thought twice about trying to fight for equality.

This truth became abundantly clear to Du Bois in Georgia, where, after graduating from Harvard in 1897, he took a position teaching in the new sociology program at Atlanta University. One day in 1899, Du

Bois was on his way to hand-deliver an op-ed to Joel Chandler Harris's Atlanta *Constitution* decrying the recent lynching in Newnan, Georgia. The black victim, Sam Hose, was murdered after he killed his employer in self-defense as a result of a heated dispute over unpaid wages. In a shocking twist, as Du Bois walked along the street that afternoon, he was horrified to see, on display in an Atlanta store window, Hose's knuckles. From that moment on, Du Bois could no longer be a detached social scientist describing empirical facts about racial inequality. He had to act. He could not bear the apathy of society at large; in fact, it truly enraged him. This is why he wasn't afraid to indict Washington's racial accommodation, going so far as to imply Washington's complicity in the 1906 Atlanta pogrom, which Du Bois's wife and young daughter barely escaped. In Du Bois's poem "A Litany of Atlanta," published in *The Independent* on October 11, 1906, the speaker says, "They told him: *Work and Rise!* . . . Yet for that man's crime this man lieth maimed and murdered, his wife naked to shame, his children to poverty and evil."[35]

Du Bois's decision to speak up was a fruitful one. In 1905, he founded the Niagara Movement, along with the radical black activist William Monroe Trotter. The movement's aim was to realize what Du Bois demands in his groundbreaking collection of essays, *The Souls of Black Folk* (1903): job opportunities, equal education, human rights, and the unfettered right to vote. "Freedom, too, the long-sought, we still seek," he writes, "the freedom of life and limb, the freedom to work and think, the freedom to love and aspire."[36]

Washington wasn't fond of Du Bois, but he despised Trotter, the young Harvard graduate whose newspaper, the *Boston Guardian*, denounced Washington as a false prophet. Trotter did the unthinkable on July 30, 1903, when he interrupted a local meeting of the National Negro Business League at the Boston AME Zion Church on Columbus Avenue, where Washington was speaking to its 258 members. Trotter, standing atop a chair, asked nine accusatory questions in protest, for instance, What were the sources of Tuskegee's secretive funding methods? Why was Washington not advocating a more militant approach to black suffrage? Trotter, after being told by the organizers to stand down and stay quiet, began to shout, "Put me out; arrest me!," before he was led off in handcuffs by police and served thirty days in jail.[37] The event, which came to be known as the "Boston Riot," enshrined Trotter as a civic radical—for he spoke truth to power. But Trotter, like Du Bois, knew the more important focus was not on personal dissent but on building a national civil rights organization that would function as a resistance movement.

But what would such an organization look like? The answer became the National Association for the Advancement of Colored People (NAACP), which Du Bois cofounded in 1909 with the white moderate Oswald Garrison Villard, who was abolitionist William Lloyd Garrison's grandson. An outgrowth of Trotter's Niagara Movement—but an organization with which Trotter wasn't involved, because he thought it was still too moderate in its reformist spirit—the NAACP was no engine of accommodation like Tuskegee. The NAACP had a racially egalitarian advocacy agenda. It fought tooth and nail President Wilson's segregation of the federal bureaucracy in the 1910s, helped black Americans serve as officers during World War I, litigated against poll taxes, and for decades pushed for federal antilynching policy.

But the truth is that the NAACP was not a revolutionary force. Civility made the NAACP work from within the system rather than change it. It took up a limited legislative approach that sought cooperation with the political establishment. And it had no comprehensive platform for gender or economic liberation.

Although she was one of the NAACP's first signatories, Ida Wells's sharp pen precluded her from sitting on its board—in the 1890s the white public met her writing with a certain level of ire. While she agreed with the NAACP's goals, Wells never did bow to its founding principle of not rocking the boat.

So she took matters into her own hands after the events in Elaine, Arkansas, on September 30, 1919, still one of the bloodiest massacres in American history. It was there that one hundred black sharecroppers who worked on white plantations attended a meeting of the Progressive Farmers and Household Union of America, led by the black Arkansas sharecropper Robert L. Hill, at a church in Phillips County. They wanted better payments for their cotton crops. After a confrontation between black security guards around the church and a white security officer who was outside turned deadly—it wasn't clear who started what, but the white officer died—one thousand white people from the adjacent areas, believing that a black insurrection was ongoing, took it upon themselves to indiscriminately slaughter any black citizen they laid eyes on. By a conservative estimate, at least several hundred black people were summarily executed.

The official story from the white power elite of Arkansas—from papers like the *Helena World* and *The Gazette*, which ran a famous headline that said "Negroes Plan to Kill All Whites"—was that the massacre was a preemptive act, meant to quash the black menace. Soon enough, after the legal system had had its say, blame was placed squarely upon the victims of white supremacy. Over 122 black people were tried, more than half of them charged with murder. After an all-white jury deliberated for all of eight whole minutes, twelve black sharecroppers, known as the "Elaine Twelve," were sentenced to the electric chair. Not one white person was prosecuted. Prominent Arkansas real estate developer E. M. Allen was overjoyed, believing justice had been done: "We have absolutely no twinge of conscience as far as the trials are concerned."[38]

But civic radicals never accept the official version of events, especially when history proves, time and time again, these stories are serviceable for power. Du Bois was incensed, writing a three-page letter to the *New York World* to argue that laying blame on both sides was preposterous, that the only "crime" the twelve Elaine sharecroppers committed was their fearless organizing against the extortion of the landlords.

Du Bois dissented from a distance, but Wells went to the scene of the crime. She came from Chicago in secret, to interview the wrongfully incarcerated men. She published her results in a pamphlet, *The Arkansas Race Riot* (1920). In it, Wells detailed the gross violation of human rights in the prison and the torture—whipping and electroshock—used by the authorities to coerce the men's confessions. She also turned the tables on the accusers by asserting that they were guilty of denying the defendants their right to due process and therefore had conspired against democracy.

With the NAACP's help and the tireless work of the black defense attorney Scipio Jones, half of the defendants were released on technical grounds by the Arkansas State Court. The rest were released after the US Supreme Court overturned their convictions in February 1923, when the court ruled that their coerced testimony and trial by an all-white jury violated the Fourteenth Amendment's equal protection clause.

The Elaine Twelve were lucky to have Ida Wells on their side. But white mobs were undeterred in their bloodlust. Soon there was another massacre, this time in Tulsa, Oklahoma, on June 1, 1921, which saw thousands of black citizens of the Greenwood section of town, known as "Black Wall Street," become refugees overnight, running for their lives half-dressed and in shock—forced out by whites who burned thirty-five city blocks and killed hundreds of people. White Tulsans were affronted by Tulsa's black citizens running their own businesses and increasing their political participation in the city. This is why, in the name of combating "civil disorder," the white Tulsa police chief, mayor, and other city officials ordered airplanes to bomb black citizens from the sky. As a former Tulsa police officer recounted later, "They gave instructions for every man to be ready and on the alert and if the niggers wanted to start anything to be ready for them. They never put forth any efforts at all to prevent it whatever, and said if they started anything to kill every b—— son of a b—— they could find."[39]

What happened in Tulsa laid bare the great irony behind Washington's call for civility: The higher black people rose socioeconomically, the more threatening they were taken to be. At the end of the day, it was white people, and they alone, who would get to decide who was respectable or not.

State-sponsored terrorism is one thing, but state inaction is just as destructive. A seventeen-year-old black teen drowned in Chicago on July 27, 1919, because white men threw stones at him while he was swimming at an unofficially segregated white beach. When the white men were not arrested, violence ensued for the next several days—twenty-three black people and fifteen white people were killed and, because of widespread and targeted arson, over one thousand black people lost their homes. In an eerie echo of President McKinley's response to Wilmington in 1898, Chicago mayor William Hale Thompson decided not to interfere and wouldn't send in police to secure the black neighborhoods. This allowed the violence to go on unabated until August 3, sending an implicit message that the black migrants arriving as part of the Great Migration from the Deep South weren't welcome up north. Chicago's white real estate agents were even more up-front, blaming the violence on what they saw as inherently lawless black migrants who were incapable of controlling their cultural tendency toward crime. Segregation in the housing market would need to continue, they said. "Reasonable restriction of leasing or selling" needed to "be enforced," they wrote, "to prevent lawlessness, destruction of values and property and loss of life."[40]

Talk of black lawlessness and interracial conflict was the perfect way for economic elites—factory owners and industrialists—to distract from the low-paying jobs at the meatpacking plants, the poor working conditions in the factories, and the extreme poverty on the city's South Side. So-called racial tension between Chicago's Irish working class and black migrants was presented by elites as more significant than their shared economic interests for better pay, safer working conditions, and equal rights. But not all were swayed by this red herring. What T. Thomas Fortune had pined for as early as the 1880s was, in fact, demonstrated on July 7, 1919, when a multiracial union marched at a local park, holding up signs that read, "The bosses think because we are of different colors and different nationalities that we should fight each other. We're going to fool them and fight for a common cause—a square deal for all."[41]

Two years earlier and three hundred miles away, in East St. Louis, Illinois, first in May and then in July 1917, white citizens killed at least thirty-nine African Americans and generated a black exodus of six thousand or more from the city. The violence took place, in part, as retaliation for black workers replacing the labor of striking white workers at the Aluminum Ore Company. The larger national conversation about abolishing an insatiable kind of capitalism was sidestepped by many elites in favor of a discussion of law and order—in other words, the concern with civility once again overshadowed the possibility of justice. Former president

Teddy Roosevelt captured the mood of the business class shortly after the events in East St. Louis, during a debate at Carnegie Hall in New York City with American Federation of Labor (AFL) president Samuel Gompers. Roosevelt gave a superficial description of the massacre and urged the audience to focus on containing disorder. In response to this "appalling outbreak of savagery," Roosevelt said that, if he were in charge, he would "put down the murderers first and investigate afterwards."[42] The message was clear to anyone paying attention: don't focus on capitalism's role in creating brutal working conditions in the aluminum plant or the reason workers were on strike to begin with—just put the bad guys in jail.

Black Americans, however, wouldn't be fooled by such an oversimplified interpretation. They knew the problem was systemic. And their response to East St. Louis was swift and seismic. Organized by the NAACP, they took to the streets in New York City on July 28, 1917, in what came to be known as the "Silent Parade." Ten to fifteen thousand people marched along Fifth Avenue in the blistering heat. Men were dressed in black, women and children in white. Together, by putting their bodies on the front line, they implied without saying a word that a hopeful vision of the future wasn't optional but essential.

Du Bois understood the power of this gesture. The events of East St. Louis were an example of the chickens coming home to roost, a product of a long history of class exploitation of both white and black workers. By the late 1910s, the socialist vision outlined by Fortune in the 1880s was beginning to assert itself in earnest in black intellectual life, and few were as committed to it as Du Bois. As he asked in his 1920 collection of essays, *Darkwater*,

> What hinders our approach to the ideals outlined above? Our profit from degradation, our colonial exploitation, our American attitude toward the Negro. Think again of East St. Louis! Think back of that to slavery and Reconstruction! Do we want the wants of American Negroes satisfied? Most certainly not, and that negative is the greatest hindrance today to the reorganization of work and redistribution of wealth, not only in America, but in the world.[43]

Du Bois had, years before, seen what socialism could do for racial equality. In 1911, he spent a year as a member of the Socialist Party of America, whose white candidate for president in 1912, Eugene V. Debs, shocked the nation when he won almost one million votes during the general election. For his part, Debs was a committed anti-racist who cofounded the Industrial Workers of the World, a union that welcomed unskilled workers and organized professions in which African Americans commonly worked. But the mainstream labor movement and the progressive movement were virtually silent on race, at best, and downright racist, at worst. Samuel Gompers and the AFL were more concerned with creating solidarity between white ethnic groups, whose antiblack racism and resentment were sometimes formative for how they saw themselves, providing them a psychological wage of superiority that they didn't get through their paychecks.

But there is no reason to concede to a democratic vision distorted by racism. One can commit to a purer vision and push others to follow suit. This is why the cooperative union Colored Farmers' National Alliance, which boasted over a million members in 1891—of which three hundred thousand were women—called for a strike of black cotton-pickers in an attempt to increase daily wages from fifty cents to one dollar. The opposition from the all-white Farmers' Alliance was fierce, and so only a few black pickers in Lee County, Arkansas, participated. The strike was crushed, and nine of the strikers were soon lynched.[44]

The next year, in 1892, New Orleans workers in the Teamsters, Scalemen, and Packers unions—known as the "Triple Alliance"—were inspired to strike in October. The New Orleans Board of Trade, which advocated for local business interests, suggested that it would only negotiate with the two all-white unions, the Scalemen and the Packers—explicitly excluding the Teamsters, who were black. But the two white unions didn't give in to the fantasy of white supremacy and abandon their black brothers. Between November 8 and November 12, twenty-five thousand workers joined the action, and the New Orleans General Strike of 1892 was born. The city was completely shut down, and the employers had no choice but to negotiate with the workers. Among their major concessions were a ten-hour workday and overtime pay.[45]

These mass actions were but a dress rehearsal for socialism, which over the next few decades was at the forefront of the civil rights struggle. Black workers were emboldened by the Bolshevik Revolution in October of 1917, which toppled the Russian monarchy, and by the growing prominence of Third World solidarity and anti-imperialist movements, which percolated after the First World War.

Black workers would crowd around Harlem street corners to hear the soapbox speeches of the black socialist Hubert Harrison. Loud and clear, he fearlessly stressed that racism was a tool of the ruling elite to fracture working-class solidarity. Black workers read with pride the poetry of Jamaican-American writer Claude McKay, who visited the Soviet Union in 1922 and acted as an unofficial delegate to the Fourth World Congress of the Communist International, where he denounced the American Communist Party's racism. Black workers read with immense interest the political and literary periodical *The Messenger*, founded in 1917 by Chandler Owen and A. Philip Randolph, which juxtaposed the fiction of Harlem Renaissance writers with advocacy for worker's rights.

Still others were drawn to more radical publications, such as *The Crusader*, written by members of the black nationalist–Marxist African Blood Brotherhood (ABB) founded by Cyril Briggs. *The Crusader* was more militant in its endorsement of black autonomy, but both *The Messenger* and *The Crusader* issued impassioned pleas for universal suffrage, worker control over the workplace, and an end to racial segregation.

This vision of an equal society was especially appealing as the Great Depression hit and unemployment skyrocketed from more than four hundred thousand in 1929 to twelve million in 1933, from 3 percent to 25 percent of the population. African Americans, in particular, knew something needed to change, so they turned to disruptive action to make their voices heard. In response to excessive landlord rent hikes and astronomically high eviction rates, 1931 saw "rent riots" in Chicago, Harlem, and Detroit, where large black crowds spontaneously gathered to prevent poor people from being made homeless by police.[46] They turned their vulnerability into anger and defiance.

But when it came to systematically organizing protests, the Communist Party of the United States of America (CPUSA), formed in 1919, was the central player. The CPUSA became well known in 1931, through its high-profile defense of the Scottsboro Boys, nine black teens wrongly accused of raping two white women aboard a freight train in northern Alabama. And through pamphlets, word of mouth, and boisterous speeches in community centers, churches, and on street corners, the CPUSA convinced poor people during the Great Depression to organize the multiracial Unemployed Councils. There were chapters in 340 cities, and by 1932, membership had reached 150,000. One of the Councils' most successful actions occurred in 1932 when, after relief aid from the government's anti-poverty program was drastically cut, it helped organize five thousand members to march straight to Chicago's relief headquarters to demand basic medical attention and three hot meals per day.[47]

Word of these activities traveled south, to one-time Alabama sharecropper and black labor organizer Hosea Hudson. After taking a ten-week course in Marxist theory sponsored by the CPUSA in 1934, Hudson returned to his home in Birmingham in 1937 to organize the Right to Vote Club, whose educational efforts quadrupled black registration in Jefferson County in several years. He racially integrated the conservative Birmingham branch of the Works Progress Administration (WPA) and became president of the United Steelworkers of America (USW) Local 2815. Under his leadership, wages tripled. But Hudson wasn't an anomaly. The radical labor movement was strong in the South. In 1934, despite threats from the Klan and warnings from police, the white socialist Norman Thomas founded the Southern Tenant Farmers' Union (STFU) in eastern Arkansas, which, within two years, had thirty-one thousand members across Texas, Missouri, Oklahoma, and Tennessee. From the beginning, the union was interracial, and through strikes and massive demonstrations, it was able to pressure President Franklin Roosevelt to establish the Farm Security Administration in 1937, after he was reelected for his second term.

Yet this high-water mark of working-class solidarity wouldn't last for long. STFU membership declined by the 1940s, and by the 1950s,

Communists like Hudson, along with countless others—of whom Paul Robeson, the black athlete, brilliant film and stage actor, and valedictorian of Rutgers College, was the most famous—were blacklisted during the Red Scare hysteria of the McCarthy era in the 1950s, when the reactionary US senator from Wisconsin, Joseph McCarthy, went on a paranoid public campaign to purge America of what he deemed were secret Communist sympathizers. Fearmongers called themselves true American patriots who wanted to take back their country. They insisted Hudson's secret goal was to create a vanguard party to overthrow the US government.

But nothing could have been further from the truth. Among other things, what civic radicals like Hudson wanted is what many Americans, especially those who proudly call themselves progressives today, would accept as a basic condition for full and equal citizenship—something that, regretfully, has still never been realized in the US. And that is, as Hudson put it, the need for, among other things, "full economic, political, and social equality to the [black] people and the right of self-determination to the [black] people in the Black Belt of the South," as well as "relief with a certain amount to all youth who could not find suitable jobs; . . . free government housing; . . . unemployed and social insurance for the old people who were too old to work; . . . equalization of education for the [black] youth in the South."[48]

To realize these progressive ideals, we must believe ordinary people are capable of extraordinary things. In his masterpiece, *Black Reconstruction in America* (1935), Du Bois illustrates this idea, providing breathtaking evidence that black emancipation happened not through Lincoln's Emancipation Proclamation of 1863 but through the actions of enslaved people themselves. Slavery crumbled through what Du Bois called the "general strike"—the minor and major revolts on the Southern plantation, the civil disobedience in the face of the master's demands, and, eventually, black soldiers taking up arms to fight for the Union Army.

The lesson of *Black Reconstruction* is that ordinary people, regardless of their formal education level or wealth, can know what is and isn't politically acceptable. This is especially true when educated policy experts—then and now—are expert at creating institutions that encourage endless war, an ever-present national security state, a mass incarceration system, and a defunded public education system, among other things. Political equality is unlike aristocracy because there is no barrier for entry. Entrance is presumed as a right and a necessity.

Du Bois died at the age of ninety-five as a card-carrying Communist, pan-Africanist, and Ghanaian citizen in self-imposed exile from America, the day before Martin Luther King Jr. gave his "I Have a Dream" speech. Since then, Du Bois's life, and especially his gravitation away from civility, has been whitewashed. During Black History Month each February, schoolchildren across the US learn about the detached, calm, composed, and respectable social scientist rather than the fierce agitator who didn't hold his tongue; they learn about the founder of the rule-abiding NAACP rather than the socialist who realized incremental reform of capitalism wasn't enough; they learn about the distinguished Harvard graduate rather than the rabble-rouser who didn't turn away from a fight when it was most necessary. The scholar is elevated above the advocate of civil disobedience, boycotts, labor strikes, and resistance to arrest.

How we understand the present hinges on what we remember about the past. And if Du Bois's work teaches us one thing, it is that remembering fierce resistance to racism helps us understand what's possible now. Racial equality isn't easily achievable. It requires strenuous work, resilience in the face of failure, and incredibly long odds.

Ida Wells brought this message to the streets. This is why in the concluding chapter of her autobiography, *Crusade for Justice* (1970), published forty years after she died, she quoted the Founding Fathers, "Eternal vigilance is the price of liberty," and she wondered if we had already stopped paying attention with the energy needed to preserve what rights we have gained. "Are [we] not too well satisfied," she asked, "to be able to point to our wonderful institutions with complacence and draw the salaries connected therewith, instead of being alert as the watchman on the wall?"[49] From the beginning of the Jim Crow era through the end of the Second

World War, the vigilant guardians of democracy were the members of the National Afro-American League; socialists, communists, feminists, and anti-lynchers. What these civic radicals knew and what we must remember is that conservatism isn't the answer, and neither is civility. What's necessary for racial justice is envisioning and building a reality that never has been but still might be.

Chapter 4

CIVIC RADICALS SPEAK
TRUTH TO POWER

On July 19, 1947, *The Nation* published a book review written by a young black writer, not yet twenty-three. The book under review, *There Was Once a Slave*, was a biography of Frederick Douglass written by the woman who would later marry W. E. B. Du Bois, Shirley Graham. In what became a characteristic trait, the reviewer, Harlem's native son, James Baldwin, extolled Graham's anti-racism but bemoaned her simplification of Douglass's complex abolitionism. Graham, in Baldwin's view, had unnecessarily sanctified Douglass, making him into an "unbelievable hero" and a "Hollywood caricature."[1]

Baldwin was no bastion of civility, and he wanted to tell the truth without any sugarcoating. He was heir both to Douglass's booming prophetic voice and Du Bois's heady intellectualism—searching yet morally clear—that left no argument unexamined. Douglass was appalled by Americans' failure to fulfill their founding commitments to equality and justice, and he blamed it on a lack of heroism. Du Bois couldn't stomach Americans' callousness. Baldwin was troubled by American convictions of purity and fantasies of innocence—romanticized historical stories that celebrated the good and ignored the horrific. Those that claimed progress was around the corner.

Everywhere Baldwin looked as a young man—whether in films star-
ring Gary Cooper or John Wayne or in popular-culture depictions of
cowboys and Indians or in the streets of Harlem, where he came of age
in the 1930s, reeling from the Great Depression—all he saw was a deficit
of love. Beneath the smiles, there was so much pain. He knew that, left
unaddressed, it would fester and destroy everything.

Baldwin couldn't stay in such a place. He was only twenty-four when
he left New York for Paris in the winter of 1948, because even New York's
Greenwich Village—where he'd found a safe haven first as a sensitive and
precocious youngster and then as a young gay man hanging with beats,
artists, musicians, and bohemians—couldn't protect him from soulless
white racism and vicious homophobia.

On July 26, 1948, while Baldwin was in Paris, Democratic president
Harry S. Truman issued an executive order to desegregate the military.
This was only three years after newly emboldened black service members
who had fought against fascism abroad came home to racial authoritarianism in the Jim Crow South. But postwar revelations of the scope of the
Nazi Holocaust had given rise to a new human rights discourse, which
resulted in the creation of the United Nations and its founding docu-
ment, the 1948 Declaration of Human Rights. In the United States, too,
changes were afoot in the conversation about race.

As Baldwin was busy in Paris, talking in cafés and bars with fellow ex-
patriates such as Richard Wright and composing his first collection of essays, *Notes of a Native Son* (1955), some white Americans began to awaken
from their moral slumber. Heartfelt white liberal narratives of conversion from racism to anti-racism emerged—white people were haunted,
shocked, and aggrieved, they said, for what they had done. These stories
had a common theme about civility and racial reconciliation: that changing white hearts and minds is key to dismantling racial inequality.

The white Georgia writer Lillian Smith spent decades running a
camp for young white girls, Laurel Falls, in the foothills of the Appala-
chian Mountains. There, from 1925 to 1948, she taught her charges about
the ills of segregation. Her memoir *Killers of the Dream* (1949), which
detailed the psychological reasons for Southern white racism, revealed to

Baldwin "a very great, and heroic, and very lonely figure."[2] As Baldwin knew, Smith paid dearly for her convictions: though she was physically unharmed, in 1955, two white kids burned down her house.

But Smith's implicit demand for racial reconciliation is something of which we must be wary. This is because it can sidestep collective responsibility and instead become about confessing individual guilt, which is no recipe for changing history. Guilt is a depressive emotion that makes one withdraw rather than take action. "We southerners had identified with the long sorrowful past on such deep levels of love and hate and guilt that we did not know how to break old bonds without pulling our lives down," Smith laments in *Killers of the Dream*. "*Change* meant leaving one's memories, one's sins, one's ambivalent pleasures."[3] The book concludes with Smith's worry that one day black leaders will "nourish their hurt dignity" on "Black Supremacy . . . Why not siphon off the tribal fury and turn it into hatred of whites?"[4]

Guilt creates anger and despair rather than hope. No one knew this better than Baldwin. A year after *Killers of the Dream* was published, his essay "Many Thousands Gone" (1950) illuminated the problem with white confessions. When white people disclose their own racism, they don't mention yet seem to expect that forgiveness will be their reward. When such forgiveness is denied, Baldwin prophesizes, white people "carried murder" in their hearts because they so desperately "wanted peace."[5] White people believe they are trying their best but grow resentful when they are not showered with gratitude by black people. This self-congratulatory aspect of white civility combines with perceptions of black incivility to fuel white grievance.

Baldwin saw both this white self-congratulation and white rage unfold during his time. The Supreme Court announced its groundbreaking decision in *Brown v. Board of Education of Topeka* (1954), which desegregated public schools, and a year later, in December 1955, the Montgomery bus boycott began when forty-two-year-old seamstress and former NAACP secretary Rosa Parks was charged with disorderly conduct for not sitting in the back of a segregated bus. White backlash quickly ensued, even from supposed allies. On March 6, 1956, a letter appeared in

Life magazine by the Nobel laureate and esteemed native son of Oxford, Mississippi, William Faulkner. Faulkner contends that if the nonviolent black freedom struggle against Jim Crow segregation doesn't "go slow," for many moderate white people, "the Negro, will now be [seen as] a segment of the topdog, and so the underdog will be that white embattled minority who are our [white people's] blood and kin."[6]

Other self-described liberals, championing individual freedom and the free market, insisted that racism would naturally be solved over time. In 1962, Milton Friedman, the libertarian University of Chicago economist and founder of the Chicago school of economics, published *Capitalism and Freedom*, a book whose argument is that the free market is the only system capable of securing political freedom and democracy. Friedman argues that racism in a liberal society committed to the rule of law is merely a matter of immoral individual acts and that it can be solved through more civil interpersonal exchanges.[7] Several years earlier in *The Economics of Discrimination* (1957), Friedman's star student, Gary Becker, then a recently minted PhD, defined racism as nothing more than a "taste." For Becker, the taste for discrimination has a burdensome cost that makes employers less competitive and allows black labor to be bought by non-racists at below market value. The idea is that racism would naturally be overcome through economic competition.[8]

Conveniently, Friedman and Becker ignore the way racism is profitable: by creating a sense of difference between black and white workers so that they don't band together and, as a result, have less power to bargain and earn higher wages. The businessman Vance Muse, a Ku Klux Klan supporter, knew this divide-and-conquer strategy well. And so he explicitly promoted "right to work" laws in Texas in 1947, which made paying union dues optional. Without such protection, Muse argued, "white women and white men will be forced into organizations with black African apes."[9]

Becker and Friedman chose to direct their anger toward anti-racist institutions and activists taking to the streets rather than toward racists like Muse. Friedman in particular railed against the fair employment practice committees—established by Franklin Roosevelt in 1941 to combat discrimination in the awarding of federal contracts—because, for him, they interfered with the freedom of any two bodies to make a contract, which he sanctified above all else. "In a society based on free discussion, the appropriate recourse is for me to seek to persuade them that their tastes are bad and that they should change their views and their behavior, not to use coercive power to enforce my tastes and my attitudes on others," he writes.[10]

In her 1963 essay "Racism," the Russian émigré and philosopher Ayn Rand—now idolized by the political right—follows suit. She introduces her condemnation of Jim Crow "racial prejudice" to set the stage for the true subject of her vitriol: black leaders who demanded affirmative action, economic justice, and school desegregation beyond the mere guarantee of equal protection under the law and full voting rights. "America has become race-conscious in a manner reminiscent of the worst days in the most backward countries of nineteenth-century Europe," she writes.[11]

Ultimately, in their rush to urge black people to be more civil, many white Americans never questioned, and actually bolstered, a dangerous idea: that racial antipathy is a natural tribal sentiment, fear is inborn, and racial preference is understandable. This became the starting point for reactionary thinking that aimed to dismantle racial progress. The New York Jewish intellectual Norman Podhoretz—who became the neoconservative editor in chief of *Commentary* magazine—in recounting his youth in a 1930s Brooklyn neighborhood in which exchanges between Jewish and black children were common, cites Baldwin as the keenest observer of racial psychology. But he criticizes Baldwin for overlooking what Podhoretz perceives as white people's "legitimate" resentment of black people. As Podhoretz explains in his 1963 essay "My Negro Problem—And Ours": "Thus, in my neighborhood in Brooklyn, I was as faceless to the Negroes as they were to me, and if they hated me because I never looked at them, I must also have hated them for never looking at me."[12]

Baldwin didn't believe in the fantasy of reverse racism peddled by segregationists or good-hearted liberals—the threat of black genocidal rage aimed at innocent whites—and neither should we. There never has been any systemic antiwhite policy in the form of slavery or segregation in the US. But the opposite is true: American history is soaked in antiblack racism. This is why Baldwin knew he had to return to the US in 1957 after seeing the venom with which young black students such as Dorothy Counts were being treated for daring to integrate formerly all-white segregated public schools in Charlotte, North Carolina, or for drinking from water fountains or for claiming space—in dance halls, at lunch counters, in movie theaters—that had long been defined in the South as for whites only. A year before, in 1956, Baldwin had published an essay in the pages of the *Partisan Review* that took direct aim at Faulkner's directive to wait. Nothing in the South's history gives evidence that there is some "future in which we will work out our salvation," Baldwin writes. "The challenge is in the moment, the time is always now."[13]

Baldwin was right in his assessment—it is impossible to believe racist structures will naturally change over time when all the historical evidence screams the opposite. This is what he describes in his masterwork of social criticism, *The Fire Next Time*. *Fire*'s publication in January of 1963 came just months before young nonviolent black activists were set upon on May 3 by officers of the Birmingham Public Safety Commission, by Eugene "Bull" Connor's dogs, by steel clubs and fire hoses; before black civil rights activist Medgar Evers was assassinated on his doorstep in Mississippi on June 12; before four little black girls were murdered by white terrorists who set a bomb on September 15 in Birmingham, Alabama's Sixteenth Street Baptist Church.

No text in all US history embodies such a moving intellectual defense of civic radical love as *Fire*. The book describes Baldwin's personal transformation from an innocent boy-preacher to a nonbeliever, from a fearful gay black teen in a white homophobic world to an artist unafraid of his feelings, from a struggling writer to a world-famous one. The book is a lesson in how white Americans need to move from innocence to freedom, from lies to truth, from defensiveness to self-examination, from cynicism to hope. The reason Baldwin's words shocked white America when they were written was that they awakened people to the disaster occurring in broad daylight, which they saw but didn't want to endow with moral salience, which they knew they were responsible for but couldn't stomach confronting. Painless reunion between white and black people is not what Baldwin counsels. What his writing demands is painful self-searching:

> Love takes off the masks that we fear we cannot live without and know we cannot live within. I use the word "love" here not merely in the personal sense but as a state of being, or a state of grace—not in the infantile American sense of being made happy but in the tough and universal sense of quest and daring and growth.[14]

For all his rhetorical fluidity, Baldwin was no grand political strategist. But Martin Luther King Jr. was. Baldwin met King in 1957 and, in a glowing profile commissioned by *Harper's* magazine in 1961, described him as exceptional. Baldwin thought it was the greatest of compliments when he said King was not to "be confused with Booker T. Washington."[15] Though Baldwin was several years older than King, Baldwin saw him as a walking God among men.

But King was no saint. In fact, he barred Baldwin from speaking at the 1963 March on Washington for Jobs and Freedom, where he delivered his most famous speech, "I Have a Dream." King thought Baldwin's sexuality would stain the movement. Had King thought more seriously about his own words and read Baldwin's more closely, he would have seen that he was applying the same standards of civility found in the white racism that he denounced.

Civility was definitely a focus throughout the civil rights movement that King led. King and his Southern Christian Leadership Council (SCLC) dressed well and turned the other cheek, no matter the brutality. King, the son of an Atlanta preacher, graduate of the Crozer Theological Seminary, and fresh PhD from Boston University, achieved national prominence when, at age twenty-six, he helped, through the Montgomery Improvement Association, organize the Montgomery bus boycott of 1955, which lasted for 381 days. Eventually King built his reputation on nonviolence and appeals to non-racist whites for solidarity with the movement throughout the 1960s.

At first glance, civility seems to be the guiding thread of "I Have a Dream." King sounds like Booker T. Washington himself when he says to avoid "drinking from the cup of bitterness and hatred" and to "conduct our struggle on the high plane of dignity and discipline." But this is just an entrée to a nineteenth-century abolitionism, which screams, "Emancipation now!" "There will be neither rest nor tranquility in America until the Negro in America is granted his citizenship rights," King says. And later, sounding like Black Lives Matter activists today, King demands an end to the "unspeakable horrors of police brutality."[16]

No surprise, then—and we must remember this now—that King thought that his "greatest stumbling block" was not the Ku Klux Klan member but the white moderate basking in civility, the rules of which dictated compromise and mutual respect.[17] This attitude was embodied in eight conservative clergymen and rabbis who, like Faulkner, despised the speed with which the black freedom struggle was moving. In an April 12, 1963, letter to King, a week into his nonviolent civil disobedience campaign in Birmingham, Alabama, the clergymen—who had earlier that year produced "An Appeal for Law and Order and Common Sense"—worried about how King's actions would lead to "hatred and violence, however technically peaceful those actions may be," and would not contribute "to the resolution of our local problems."[18]

Ironically, these clergymen and longtime FBI director J. Edgar Hoover had similar views of King, in spite of their different political views. Hoover began monitoring King as early as 1956 as part of his Racial Matters program, because he believed King was "a secret member of the Communist Party." In a November 1964 press conference, after Hoover had determined that King's rule-breaking boycotts were a danger to national security, he called King the "most notorious liar in the country."[19]

The reason the moderate clergymen and Hoover were afraid of King was that he didn't back away from disruptive direct action. We're often encouraged to exclusively remember King's nonviolence and Christian humility, but the crown jewel of his legacy is his civic radicalism—showing how getting out in the streets, collectively and directly, makes people in power listen closely and carefully. Elites didn't want the Southern economy to be boycotted, black women to forgo their domestic and secretarial work, young people to miss school, and the public square to become another kind of school.

But this is exactly what happened. The day after Rosa Parks was jailed, Jo Ann Robinson—a black English teacher and head of the Women's Political Council of Montgomery—distributed fifty thousand leaflets to businesses, barbershops, and schools to organize for black freedom. The Montgomery bus boycott of 1955 was but a dress rehearsal for the Greensboro, North Carolina, sit-in of February 1, 1960, during which four black men, dressed in suits, sat in the "whites only" section of the restaurant in Woolworth department store. Their courageous act set off a firestorm and inspired similar moves in Hampton, Virginia; Rock Hill, South Carolina; and Little Rock, Arkansas. At Booker T.'s pride and joy, Tuskegee University, three hundred protesters fearlessly marched downtown in solidarity with nine black students who had been expelled from neighboring Alabama State University after they sat at a "whites only" lunch counter in the basement of the Montgomery County courthouse on February 25, 1960. On March 15 of that year, in Atlanta, two hundred black students stormed ten different segregated restaurants.

The following year, in 1961, the Freedom Rides began. A multiracial group of students descended upon the South in buses to occupy segregated bus terminals, bathrooms, and rest areas in Alabama, Mississippi, Louisiana, and South Carolina. These youngsters were met with open hostility almost everywhere they traveled. On May 14, a mob of forty whites from Anniston, Alabama, surrounded one of their buses, slashing its tires and throwing rocks at its windows. Reporters who witnessed the event were treated as anti-racist conspirators—one was beaten, his camera smashed. Another bus escaped the wreckage in Anniston and made its way to Birmingham later that day, where thirty locals were waiting with lead pipes and bicycle chains. The police, headed by Birmingham Safety Commissioner Bull Connor, were five minutes away but did nothing to stop the assaults. When an FBI agent arrived, he couldn't make out the Freedom Riders' faces because they were drenched in blood. Commissioner Connor's explanation was that it was Mother's Day, and many officers were off duty.[20] A more obvious reason explains the police force's inaction in Montgomery, Alabama: most of the members of the force were affiliated with or at least sympathetic to the Klan.[21]

The fire and militancy the Freedom Riders espoused, despite the reactionary backlash they generated, came from the same wellspring of commitment from which King drank. This commitment to equality and justice is why King was always revolutionary and why it is impossible for him to only be seen as preaching "racial empathy," of simply appreciating different viewpoints about racial identity and how it affects all people. When King said in his "Letter from a Birmingham Jail" (1963), "Injustice anywhere is a threat to justice everywhere," he was talking about combating the antiblack racism of Jim Crow, not some imagined antiwhite racism enacted by black people. Period. This is why King was arrested and jailed in Birmingham on Good Friday, April 12, 1963, along with Ralph Abernathy, for violating the ban on marching, which was put in place by the city and ultimately upheld by the Alabama state circuit court on April 10, 1963, for the declared purpose of public safety. What King called *agape*—an ancient Greek term defined as love—was an emancipatory force, attacking hierarchies using methods beyond what is acceptable as a matter of decorum. Breaking the law "lovingly," as King puts it in his letter, is the only choice when the law is unjust.

A year before, in December 1962, when he was arrested and jailed in Albany, Georgia, rather than pay a $178 fine for illegally protesting, King had awakened to the way white supremacists skillfully co-opted civility for their own purposes. The friendly red-haired Albany police chief, Laurie Pritchett, strategically joined black activists in prayer before arresting them and brought reporters to sites where police were showing restraint with protesters, rather than to the sites where they were unleashing violence upon them.

White supremacists hid behind civility to distract from their iron clubs, while white liberals used it to justify their inaction. James Baldwin saw this latter dynamic firsthand when he, along with a group of other distinguished black figures—including his brother David, playwright Lorraine Hansberry, Freedom Rider Jerome Smith, the actors and singers

Lena Horne and Harry Belafonte, and psychologist Kenneth Clark, who was there in place of King—visited with the US attorney general, Robert Kennedy, on May 24, 1963, at his New York home. Bobby's brother, John F. Kennedy, the sitting president, and the administration he led were in no rush to push hard on civil rights legislation. The president privately bristled at the negative publicity the Freedom Rides aroused.[22]

At the meeting with Bobby Kennedy, Baldwin joined the chorus of voices pushing the administration to take a forceful federal stand against Jim Crow, asking that the president personally escort a black child to a segregated Southern school. This symbolized a "moral commitment," they believed, that would send a clear and unmistakable message. But Bobby politely declined on JFK's behalf, and, to Baldwin's surprise, instead became increasingly annoyed and prickly and began lecturing them about the art of political compromise. When Jerome Smith, who had been viciously beaten on a Freedom Ride, expressed his disgust that the meeting needed to happen in the first place, Bobby was taken aback. In an effort to redirect the conversation and create common ground, Bobby pointed to his personal story—he was a son of Irish immigrants—to say that black progress was just a matter of time, that upward mobility through hard work was on the horizon. To which Baldwin responded that time was running out for the federal government to address black grievances. Lorraine Hansberry had had enough, so she stormed out in protest. The rest of the group soon followed, knowing what civic radicals know: declarations of goodwill are cheap, toothless expressions of solidarity useful for winning elections but nothing more than that.[23]

As the years wore on, Baldwin's lecturing, marching, teaching and writing were motivated by wanting to show Americans how intellectual growth and moral awakening are not independent of but enmeshed in politics. Baldwin once confessed that he despised Harriet Beecher Stowe's *Uncle Tom's Cabin*, calling it "a very bad novel . . . in its self-righteous, virtuous sentimentality."[24] But, in truth, his own artistic goal was to create a moral sentiment worthy of free Americans. As a towering wordsmith, Baldwin stirred the youth, who flocked to his lectures. Coming of age in the 1960s, when the counterculture made anything possible—free love, antiwar activism, feminism, the sexual revolution, gay liberation, socialism, rock 'n' roll—young people truly felt alive to act with sense of purpose, to forge a new consciousness as the world shifted beneath their feet.

Baldwin didn't always get it right, betraying his own message with his behavior. At times, he seemed to defend civility when he was aggrieved by the militant tactics of young activists. In 1964, he didn't get behind a stall-in led by the Brooklyn Congress of Racial Equality (CORE) to prevent entry into the New York State Pavilion during its World Fair, because, as he said, "the country is already so congested nobody can get anywhere anyway."[25]

But Baldwin's words had a life of their own. Making youth believe in something greater than themselves that is worth fighting for is as critical as movement building. One student who read Baldwin closely was University of Michigan undergraduate Tom Hayden. Hayden's influential organization, Students for a Democratic Society, and the democratic socialist manifesto it published, the Port Huron Statement (1962), told young middle-class white radicals on college campuses who came of age believing in the American dream that there was a close connection between antiblack racism, the exploitation of working people's labor, and rule by politicians held hostage by corporate interests. Another white middle-class student influenced by Baldwin was Mario Savio, who became a spokesperson for the Free Speech Movement when he protested the University of California–Berkley administration's ban on student political activity—put in place not long after four hundred students occupied the Sheraton Palace hotel on campus, which was accused of racially discriminatory hiring practices. On October 1, 1964, Savio organized a spontaneous thirty-hour sit-in around a police car and gave an impassioned speech. This experience transformed Savio, proving to him that "once that hurdle is overcome, of physically structuring the possibility for a community," activists become bound together, not just politically but socially.[26] The Free Speech Movement, of which Savio was a leader, was instrumental in ending the Vietnam War by encouraging resistance to the draft; in pushing for multicultural, anti-racist and gender studies university courses reflective of the student body; and in questioning the organization of the workplace and the need for a nuclear family.

Activists associated with the student movement saw space (the university classroom or the factory floor, the rural county or the city street) as a platform to visualize popular power and challenge the authority of bosses, managers, and professors. Their occupation of university buildings put emancipation front and center, rather than allowing the administrators to frame the conversation about what kind of college education is appropriate. This tactic of occupation is also what led to the creation of the first Black Studies program at San Francisco State University in 1968, and over six hundred similar programs by 1973. The student movement did not simply air grievances of hurt feelings but politicized the Eurocentric curriculum to include denigrated black perspectives.

Young activists in the 1960s put democracy into practice for dispossessed people who weren't invited to join the conversation in the public sphere. Hayden and Savio became personally involved in the black liberation struggle after joining Freedom Summer in 1964, a massive effort to register tens of thousands of black Mississippians to vote, organized by the Student Nonviolent Coordinating Committee (SNCC). Too confrontational and shrill was how some white moderates described SNCC. But SNCC's members had no choice but to be bold, given that they operated within the deadly territory of the Deep South—in Mississippi, Georgia, and Tennessee—where racial violence was the defining feature of the social sphere.

But nothing comes cheap. While the Voter Registration Project, headed by the young black Harvard University graduate, Robert "Bob" Moses, would register five hundred thousand across the South, in Mississippi it added only four thousand. Nearly four hundred thousand black people went unregistered there. Here is why: In McComb, Mississippi, in 1961, a Democratic state legislator shot a black man to death for ignoring his warning not to register to vote. He was acquitted after the all-white jury ruled the killing was a justifiable homicide. In August 1962, when Fannie Lou Hamer—who would become an iconic black feminist, orator, and civil rights activist—registered to vote in Indianola, Mississippi, after attending her first SNCC event, she was fired from a sharecropping job she had held for eighteen years. Then, in September, when word got around about Hamer's political activities, white terrorists shot sixteen bullets into the home of her friend Mary Tucker, where Hamer had been staying for some time. Hamer had already left to go north to Tallahatchie County, but the bullets went through the wall where her head would have been had she been sleeping there.

SNCC activists were undeterred by such violence. They created their own community from scratch where there had been none. And no one is as exemplary a model for contemporary organizing as SNCC's leading theoretical voice, analyst, motivation, and catalyst—Ella Baker. Baker had a stint as a secretary with Martin Luther King's SCLC, but she later became the inspiration for both Bob Moses and Stokely Carmichael—who popularized the slogan "Black Power." Baker was a throwback to Harriet Tubman rather than to Frederick Douglass. Moses and Carmichael—like other SNCC activists—heard stories about how Baker was the chief organizer of a three-day convention at Raleigh, North Carolina, on April 16, 1960, which featured students sharing their experiences and coordinating actions. Baker appreciated the agency, self-knowledge, and desire for justice that burned in the illiterate sharecroppers who toiled endlessly, only to be trapped in poverty and powerlessness. She phoned families of young SNCC activists who were jailed. And with whatever donations and funds were available from supporters and members, Baker set up scholarships for those expelled from school and provided money to cover medical expenses for those who needed it.

SNCC activists, mentored by Baker, knew political consciousness is essential for action. The SNCC Freedom Schools, launched by a class facilitated by Staughton Lynd on July 4, 1964, analyzed the roles white supremacy, labor relations, and black enslavement played in the perpetuation of racist systems. The class facilitators used the Socratic method and conversation as their main teaching strategies. And students were given the opportunity to articulate why voting rights and equal protection under the law were basic foundations for citizenship. By the end of the summer, they would take what they had learned to twenty-five sites and share it with 2,500 black schoolchildren, adults, and seniors from all walks of life.

While some SNCC leaders were busying politicizing black Southerners, others wanted to help sympathetic white people across the nation visualize what segregation looked like. This was the purpose behind a fifty-four-mile march from Selma to Montgomery, Alabama. The march started on March 7, 1965, when an interracial crowd of six hundred gathered at Brown Chapel African Methodist Church. The Reverend King had described the march as too risky and declined to join because of the difficult walking conditions along stretches of empty road conducive to acts of white racial terror.

But the march's SNCC leader, John Lewis, thought the rewards of the march would outweigh the dangers, for it would shine a bright spotlight on the brutal system of white supremacy against which black people and their allies were fighting. Lewis was right, even though the march succeeded at a huge personal cost to him. As he led the marchers across the Edmund Pettus Bridge, state troopers in gas masks, led by Major John Cloud, unleashed tear gas and began pummeling the participants with batons and bare fists. Before long, troopers had knocked five women unconscious and fractured Lewis's skull. Reporters extensively covered the event, which would be known as "Bloody Sunday."

No one could look away from the carnage in good faith. Not even President Lyndon Johnson, the lanky, domineering, brash Democrat from Texas who always seemed to be itching for a fight. Unlike Kennedy, Johnson was not one to question his own skill at bargaining or his talent for persuasion. But the decade-long grassroots movement, beginning with the Montgomery bus boycott in 1955, had pushed him and other elites into a corner.

Johnson had already signed the Civil Rights Act of 1964, which outlawed racial discrimination and ensured the federal guarantee of equal protection. But now was the time to do something even more significant. Within two weeks of the Selma Campaign, Johnson urged Congress to pass the more comprehensive Voting Rights Act, which was drafted on March 19, 1965. Two days later, King led another march from Selma to

Montgomery—3,200 turned into 25,000 after four days of walking. James Baldwin was among the marchers, walking hand in hand with the singer Joan Baez. After a summer of debate, the Voting Rights Act was passed on August 3, 1965, in the US House 328–74 and the next day in the Senate by a margin of 77–19. The new law dismantled Jim Crow disenfranchisement, finally winning black Southerners the right to vote. Section 5 of the legislation, in particular, required Southern states to get preclearance and approval from the federal government, specifically the US attorney general, on any electoral changes they would make to their voting processes.

Despite this indication of real political progress, the Voting Rights Act did nothing to alleviate the everyday struggles in urban neighborhoods, such as Harlem, where Baldwin had grown up and where the majority of black working-class people made their home. Five days after Americans celebrated what in retrospect appears to be the high-water mark of the civil rights movement, Baldwin was hardly surprised when he heard the news of an eruption in the Watts neighborhood of Los Angeles on August 11, 1965. The fire next time, which he had predicted two years earlier in his book with that title, had arrived.

A white police officer, Lee Minikus, arrested a twenty-one-year-old black man, Marquette Frye, for drunk driving, and their tense exchange quickly escalated on that ninety-eight-degree summer evening. A crowd gathered to watch, more police arrived, and soon yelling from the crowd became rock throwing, which turned into full-out war of residents versus police officers. Watts erupted in flames. The fuse had been lit on a powder keg created by white racism. The 250,000 black citizens of Watts were squeezed into a segregated area where trash was rarely collected, where unemployment was at 34 percent, and where the police department was almost entirely white. Watts wasn't an anomaly—if you visited the black neighborhoods of Chicago, New York, Memphis, or Detroit, you'd see something similar. After six days of flames caused by arson, the damage in Watts was conservatively estimated at $45 million. Fourteen thousand National Guard and thousands of local police were mobilized to squash the disturbance. Thirty-four people were killed, over one thousand injured, and almost four thousand arrested. Hundreds were left homeless.[27]

Similarly, on July 12, 1967, in Newark, New Jersey, police beat a black cab driver, and 150 urban black rebellions erupted across the nation and raged for four days. Twenty-six people died and hundreds were injured. In the early morning hours of July 23 in Detroit, Michigan, the city police—from a force that was over 90 percent white—raided an unlicensed club on Twelfth Street in a black neighborhood, and soon the city exploded. When things settled on July 28, forty-three people were dead and seven thousand arrests had been made.[28] The Motor City had been turned into a battlefield, replete with tanks crawling across the roads and National Guardsmen equipped with machine guns roaming the streets.

As a result of these events, a narrative emerged to describe urban rebellion as a product of black cultural pathology. The distinguished historian at Harvard University Oscar Handlin told the *New York Times* that the events in Watts were a product of "disorderly elements" who were looking to loot anything and everything in sight.[29] And the writer Theodore White explained another uprising—the Harlem uprising from July 16 to July 22, 1964—as a product of black "biological anarchy."[30] Six days of rage erupted after an NYPD police lieutenant, Thomas Gilligan, shot and killed a fifteen-year-old African American teen, James Powell, in broad daylight and in front of his friends, on suspicion of harassing a white superintendent of an apartment complex. Theodore White didn't see the Harlem uprising as the result of built-up frustration over police brutality, poverty, crumbling housing, asbestos-filled buildings, and defunded schools. What he saw instead was the rise of "junior savages," from "broken homes and loveless breeding warrens."[31]

This reasoning wasn't new. It had its roots in 1940s social science. It was then that a generation of policymakers known as "racial liberals" were influenced by the Swedish social scientist Gunnar Myrdal's mammoth 1,483-page study, *An American Dilemma: The Negro Problem and Modern Democracy* (1944), which argues that, after centuries of enslavement and Jim Crow, black culture

> is a distorted development, or a pathological condition, of the general American culture . . . We assume that it is to the advantage of American

Negroes as individuals and as a group to become assimilated into American culture, to acquire the traits held in esteem by the dominant white Americans.[32]

From the 1940s onward, these so-called racial liberals were careful to unequivocally assign blame for racial inequality to white racism, not black irresponsibility. They made this argument because, in their view, it helped create public sympathy to expand affirmative action programs, desegregate public schools, and eliminate racist housing policies. The doll study conducted by black psychologists Kenneth Clark and Mamie Clark highlighted the psychological effects of racism on black children, and Kenneth Clark's testimony persuaded the Supreme Court to rule against public segregation in *Brown v. Board*. When presented with a choice, the Clarks' research concluded, most black children wanted dolls with white skin and associated dolls with black skin with ugliness.

But by the 1960s, results of social science studies were being used to explain broken homes, alcoholism, and criminality. The text that introduced this argument to the broader public was written by Harvard sociologist Daniel Patrick Moynihan, then the assistant secretary of labor under President Johnson (he would go on to become a US senator from New York and was one of the longest-serving, from 1977 to 2001). Moynihan's internal report for the Johnson administration, *The Negro Family: The Case for National Action* (1965), which was eventually released to and widely discussed by the public, claimed that a lack of a strong fatherly presence in the black nuclear household created what Moynihan called the "tangle of pathology" of limited wealth and chronic underemployment.

For Baldwin, such arguments were distortions at best and racist ramblings at worst. What is necessary, he said, is to think historically and dispense with the lies of American exceptionalism being fed to us. Baldwin delivered this message to the students who gathered to watch him debate American race relations with the founder of the conservative *National Review*, William F. Buckley, at Cambridge University on February 18, 1965. What they heard Baldwin say is what one would never say in polite company: slavery had made the American dream possible, and the urban eruptions came from a long history of white supremacy.[33] The 1950s of white picket fences in white suburbs offered no such ease for black citizens. They were subject to what came to be known as "redlining," which is to say, they were excluded from various neighborhoods and denied home mortgage loans by banks that, in racially coded language, categorized them as "high risk." White people got loans simply by being white. America, Baldwin said, called itself a civil country and supposedly championed freedom, but it was "full of the corpses of [his] ancestors." He was flabbergasted that his "freedom" and his "citizenship" were questioned. Until Americans accepted that "I am one of the people who built the country," he continues, "there is scarcely any hope for the American dream."[34]

We need more of Baldwin's rejoinders today. His words to Buckley about the American Dream dismantled a burgeoning line of reasoning that was in its infancy but would be mainstream by the 1970s. Newly discovered white ethnic identities (Italian American, Polish American, Jewish American, German American) of immigrants who came to the US in the late nineteenth and early twentieth centuries were used to undercut affirmative action and integrated busing programs in Boston, Cleveland, and Long Island, New York. What historian Matthew Frye Jacobson calls "white ethnic revival" became a way to say, My ancestors didn't enslave black people or profit from Jim Crow, so why should my hard-earned tax dollars be used for "preferential" treatment for blacks?[35]

Norman Podhoretz, editor of *Commentary*, openly wonders, "What share had they [Italian and Jewish immigrants]—downtrodden people themselves breaking their own necks to eke out a living—in the exploitation of the Negro?"[36] Similarly, in his 1972 book *The Rise of the Unmeltable Ethnics*, Michael Novak, the neoconservative intellectual and professor of religious studies and philosophy at the State University of New York at Old Westbury, shares a personal anecdote about hearing a Native American on a subway platform tell Polish nuns that they had exterminated his ancestors. Novak then comments that his ancestors, who had only escaped European serfdom themselves four generations before, "never saw an Indian . . . Nor were they responsible for enslaving the blacks."[37] The idea that white people aren't responsible for addressing systemic racism, combined with widespread white fear of black unruliness, gave rise to "white flight" from large cities like Detroit, Newark, and Atlanta to their adjoining suburbs. Percolating since the 1950s, this demographic shift peaked in the late 1960s. Suburbs became increasingly homogenous, white, securitized, and Republican, while black cities were defunded and left to ruin.

Had Podhoretz or Novak truly understood the argument of Baldwin's *Fire*, they might have been struck by the fact that they themselves were the perfect embodiment of the white innocence Baldwin lamented. Ignored in their revisionist histories that black people's problems were caused by black pathology was what Baldwin knew wasn't considered patriotic or respectable to say: white ethnics, unlike black people, could easily pass as Anglo-Saxon Protestants by changing their last names, and they would never deal with antiblack racism when they filled out job applications, went on job interviews, or applied for home loans.

Moreover, as political scientist Ira Katznelson points out, there was a time when affirmative action was white. Democratic president Franklin Delano Roosevelt's New Deal in the 1930s and 1940s was designed to be beneficial "almost exclusively for whites."[38] Implementing New Deal programs state-by-state kept happy the racist Southerners who were part of Roosevelt's Democratic governing coalition, while empowering local businesses and politicians to exclude black citizens to the fullest extent possible. For instance, the social programs associated with the Social Security Act of 1935 were specifically made unavailable to maids and farmers, many of whom were black and living in the rural Deep South. Moreover, the GI Bill, passed in 1944, aimed to help returning World War II veterans gain access to home loans and stipends to cover college education. But black veterans couldn't take advantage of them because of racism. Banks deemed these veterans more likely to default on their loans than their white counterparts in similar socioeconomic circumstances. And for many black veterans, tuition assistance for college meant little, given that many universities were segregated or had only small black student populations.

This condition of socioeconomic inequality, along with widespread police brutality against unarmed black men and women, was why black people couldn't take it anymore—and angrily took the streets in Watts, Newark, and Detroit. No one knew this better than Baldwin, who wrote in *Ebony* magazine in 1965, "The great force of history comes from the fact that we carry it within us, are unconsciously controlled by it in many ways, and history is literally *present* in all that we do."[39]

Martin Luther King Jr. agreed. And as the 1960s wore on, he increasingly abandoned civility as a strategy. His denunciations of American apathy were fiercer, his critique of capitalism bolder, and his rebuke of American imperialism in Vietnam intensified. Recognizing that President Johnson and the Democrats were unwilling to go beyond granting equal protection under the law and were terrified of economic justice, King sounded more and more like other activists commonly presented as his antithesis: the young black militants affiliated with Black Power. In private conversations with one of them, Stokely Carmichael, he worried that the term "black power" had connotations of black supremacy, which would alienate sympathetic whites who, in principle, shared the goal of eliminating black poverty. But at same time, King shared Carmichael's view that fighting poverty was central to the black freedom movement.

To make good on this vision and organize black citizens in the Midwest, King, in January 1966, moved his family to an apartment in Chicago's North Lawndale neighborhood on the west side of the city, known colloquially as "Slumdale." When King first stepped into the apartment on South Hamline Street, he was overwhelmed by the stench of urine, the bedbugs, and the large rats—defining features of many of the homes in that area. When he spoke to young people in the streets, he sensed their unmistakable hopelessness. The neighborhood featured a lack of jobs, an overabundance of gang activity, and scant community resources. At times it felt to King like a war zone rather than a neighborhood. North Lawndale was only twelve miles away from the University of Chicago, where Milton Friedman was busy, from the security of the ivory tower, predicting to his students the eventual eradication of racism through an increase in white civility.

But good manners don't change bad policies. So, on February 23, King convinced several families in the building in which he lived to with-hold rent, which was the opening salvo for his July 10 Freedom Sunday at Chicago's Soldier Field stadium, which brought together thirty thousand people and was aimed at encouraging black and Puerto Rican residents to unite in a boycott against banks, local companies, and real estate agents.

However, it became clear that King was making more enemies than friends in Chicago during his stay there. The Democratic Chicago mayor, Richard J. Daley, thought that King was openly encouraging theft in the city's residents and that he secretly wanted Chicago to become the next Watts. For their part, black Chicago youth, unlike their parents, were fed up with King's soaring Christian rhetoric and wanted immediate change. So they mercilessly booed him when he spoke to them. Their growing impatience had been illustrated a month earlier, in June, when King joined Stokely Carmichael in the March Against Fear. The march, organized by James Meredith—a black US Air Force veteran and the first black student to desegregate the University of Mississippi, on October 2, 1962—would take the participants from Memphis, Tennessee, to Jackson, Mississippi. Meredith was shot and injured by a white mob on the second day of the march, and by the time King and Carmichael confronted another mob in Canton, Mississippi, Carmichael had had enough. Nonviolence was difficult, if not downright impossible, faced with such terror. King wasn't naïve. He understood the stakes, confessing that, seeing firsthand the un-controllable white rage in Canton, "I sure did not want to close my eyes when we prayed."[40]

But the pragmatic question of violence versus nonviolence—then, as always—is for the civic radical far less important than the necessity of pushing for greater freedom. Back in Chicago, on August 5, 1966, King marched with six hundred activists to Marquette Park, where he saw the children of white ethnic immigrants—Poles, Italians, Germans—chanting "Hate!," brandishing Confederate flags, wearing Nazi regalia, and throwing rocks at his fellow marchers. King barely dodged a knife thrown at him. This wasn't the Deep South but the state Abraham Lincoln had once called home. The event shook King to the bone, but he persisted. After he threatened to march to the lily-white Chicago suburb of Cicero—a sundown town where the residents' racism was only thinly veiled—Mayor Daley became worried about the outbreak of full-out war. So he agreed to enforce Chicago's open-housing policy, which aimed to ban racist discrimination against prospective black renters, and to increase the number of low-cost public housing units in the city, while directly working with banks to ensure that potential black homeowners had greater access to mortgages.

In the grand scheme of things, Daley's concessions weren't worth much. But they still testified to King's changing understanding of what the freedom struggle would ultimately require. He captured this revelation in his sermon "Where Do We Go from Here?" delivered to SCLC on August 16, 1967:

> Now, we got to get this thing right. What is needed is a realization that power without love is reckless and abusive, and that love without power is sentimental and anemic. Power at its best is love implementing the demands of justice, and justice at its best is love correcting everything that stands against love. And this is what we must see as we move on.
>
> . . . The problem indicates that our emphasis must be twofold: We must create full employment, or we must create incomes.[41]

King reminds us here that socioeconomic resources are crucial for building a democratic society whose citizens are capable of self-determination. From the perspective of the ruling class, nothing was civil about King's demand for the abolition of poverty in this speech, which set the stage for his multiracial Poor People's Campaign that began in earnest on May 12, 1968, in Washington, DC. It was there that activists demanded an Economic Bill of Rights from the federal government and a $30 billion investment in an anti-poverty program. What they demanded—a living wage, more affordable housing, and full employment—was a threat to the ruling class because it required higher taxes on the rich and empowered working people to make decision for themselves. Baldwin knew this too. As early as January 12, 1961, he spoke at a Harlem rent strike organized by the Rent Coordinating Committee, which eight hundred people attended. There, Baldwin said, "It isn't only the landlord you have to fight, it is also the insurance companies [who profit from black debt]."[42]

In his demands for economic justice, King had more in common than we would ever admit with the organization that Baldwin eventually supported in the late 1960s, the Black Panther Party for Self-Defense, founded in 1966 by Huey P. Newton and Bobby Seale in response to over-policing and police brutality in Oakland, California. Their rebellious spirit resonated with Baldwin, even if he felt uneasy about their homophobia and militarism. He attended multiple Black Panther fundraisers in Oakland and became close with Newton after he was released from prison in 1970—for allegedly killing a white Oakland Police Department officer, John Frey, who had stopped Newton's vehicle for suspicious activity on October 28, 1967. Baldwin was a frequent visitor to the Huey Newton School in Oakland and wrote the introduction to Seale's 1970 autobiography, *Seize the Time*.

By the late 1960s, many white liberals were outraged by the rising tide of black radicalism. In his well-received memoir, *North Toward Home* (1967), the *Harper's* magazine editor Willie Morris—chronicling his transformation from Southern white racist in Mississippi to liberal intellectual in New York—took for granted the efficacy of the black freedom movement. But he still had an axe to grind with the ideological militants who he thought distracted from its cause. Morris thought Faulkner was the most penetrating interpreter of the Southern mind, a "prophet of the human soul," and he also counted Baldwin's earliest essays as among his favorites.[43] Morris's elevation of centrist black intellectuals who saw American society in a redemptive light—Ralph Ellison, who wrote the classic novel *Invisible Man* (1952), and the cultural critic Albert Murray, author of *The Omni-Americans* (1970)—said as much about what he loved as what he despised. Ellison and Murray, as Morris put it in *North Toward Home*, "refused to view their own Southern past apocalyptically, as if it had all been disaster."[44]

Morris yearned for less bitter black leaders who could appreciate the complexity of the Southern past. But a more nefarious paranoia about black incivility was evident in Larry L. King's sobering memoir, *Confessions of a White Racist* (1971), which was a finalist for the National Book Award and was praised by, among many intellectuals, the black poet Maya Angelou. Larry King was incensed about increasing black militancy in the form of Black Power, which demanded self-determination, democratic participation, and autonomy. In his writing, competing black ideologies, sources of discontent, and freedom dreams are effaced. As King writes, "It scares us to death.... I am judged by blacks as arbitrarily as I once judged them ... becoming more suspicious, more ingrown, more tribal, more cautious, more fearful."[45] White liberals, their hopes for racial harmony betrayed, nosedived into frightening nightmares of race war.

If Larry King was thinking about the Panthers when he wrote this, he probably had an image of them walking lockstep with shotguns strapped across their chests, berets tilted, and fists raised. But the lasting insight of the Panthers isn't the politics of self-defense but this: to oppose police brutality and mass incarceration against people of color, we cannot just enact reforms to these institutions, but we must create a new community in which people are treated as ends rather than means. This is what the Panthers did with their "survival programs," which were extraordinary in their ambition and scope—no-cost breakfast for schoolchildren, soup kitchens, liberation schools, free shoes, medical research clinics for sickle cell anemia, loan programs, ambulance services, prison transportation, land banking, free clothing, employment assistance, and pest control services. The civic radical knows that we need citizenship not based on profit-maximization but on treating the whole person with dignity. We must create a public philosophy in which severe economic exploitation isn't tolerated and people's freedom to live fulfilling lives isn't thrown into the gutter.

In the late 1960s, few were more committed to realizing this kind of citizenship than Detroiters Grace Lee Boggs and her partner, the Chrysler plant autoworker and black political theorist James (Jimmy) Boggs. Grace, who knew James Baldwin from her time in New York in the 1940s, must have seen something incredibly poignant in his staunch humanism. But, unlike Baldwin, Grace and Jimmy were community organizers rather than artists. They were more prescient than Baldwin in knowing that post-industrialization was quickly transforming work into something more precarious and less reliable for millions of people. Technological improvement, Jimmy insists in his classic but still underappreciated *The American Revolution: Pages from a Negro Worker's Notebook* (1963), only creates opportunities for greater markets into which capitalism can sink its teeth. As a result, workers must "stop shirking responsibility and start assuming responsibility," stop acting like "a bunch of ants" who "can't decide how to distribute" their wealth and "fight among themselves and destroy each other to get at the accumulation."[46]

One of Jimmy Boggs's mentees in Detroit, General Baker, organized the Dodge Revolutionary Union Movement (DRUM) in 1968 in the Polish neighborhood of Hamtramck. The goal was to transform the local Dodge plant, which was under white leadership even though 70 percent of its workforce was black. Through a series of spontaneous wildcat strikes orchestrated by workers from below without sanction from the union leaders, DRUM demanded an end to discrimination and greater black leadership in the United Auto Workers. The strikes sparked the formation of the short-lived League of Revolutionary Black Workers in 1969, whose impact was minor in terms of policy changes but major in terms of its critique of progressivism. DRUM put into practice what Baldwin, Grace, and Jimmy believed: Revolution is not about reorganizing government to be more representative or redistributing private property but rather about changing how we relate to one another. It is about giving up the quest for ever-greater wealth and boldly dreaming a future that benefits everyone and inventing ways such a future can be made possible.

Another revolutionary dreamer was Detroit Red, born Malcolm Little in Omaha, Nebraska, in 1925 and later known as Malcolm X. When Malcolm was two, his father, Earl Little, a fierce and vocal supporter of Marcus Garvey's black nationalist philosophy of black self-empowerment and self-sufficiency, moved his wife and children to Lansing, Michigan, to escape the Klan. But it was there, when Malcolm was six, that Earl

Little was murdered by local whites, who threw him to his death under a streetcar. The death was deemed a suicide, so the family couldn't collect on Earl Little's life insurance policy. Soon after, Malcolm's mother, Louise, began to spiral into depression, and, in 1937, she was placed in the Kalamazoo psychiatric hospital. Malcolm and his siblings were sent to different foster homes.

Early in his life, Malcolm wasn't the political activist that we remember now. He grew up to be, by turns, a gangster, a hustler, and a pimp. But he changed in a major way when he was introduced to Nation of Islam (NOI) teachings when he was in a Massachusetts jail from 1946 to 1952 for larceny. The Nation of Islam stressed Islamic rather than Christian teachings, aligning Islam with the spiritual roots of the African diaspora worldwide. From the Nation, Malcolm learned about black pride, black solidarity, and consciousness-raising, and he began to denounce Christianity, which he perceived as encouraging a mentality of submission and humility in the face of white racism. Malcolm became a devout convert and evangelical, spreading the gospel of salvation he had learned from the Black Muslim organization and its leader, Elijah Muhammad, who notoriously described white people as "devils" to his ten thousand registered followers and roughly fifty thousand sympathizers.

Not all of Malcolm's ideas are worth recovering in the here and now. Early in his career, what saved Malcolm also made him complicit in spreading religious ideas about rigid moral virtue, black supremacy, abstinence, and teetotalism, ideas that could prevent activists from building a broad-based movement. Black self-determination is an attractive idea, but in the Nation of Islam it was forced to coexist alongside misogyny and homophobia. Powerful elites who unilaterally claim that divine providence gives them the authority to speak for the masses must be treated with suspicion. And Muhammad, like Booker T. Washington before him, went to great lengths to preserve his ironclad grip over his people, in this case, NOI temples and their congregants across Chicago, Hartford, Atlanta, and Detroit.

By the early 1960s, Malcolm's reverence for Elijah Muhammad's authority began to crumble. So silence wasn't an option for him after he learned of President John F. Kennedy's assassination by Lee Harvey Oswald in Dallas, Texas. In describing that fateful day as the "chickens coming home to roost," Malcolm portrayed the murder of Kennedy as an extension of longstanding American apathy over black ghettoization; the CIA's overthrow of the democratically elected president of Congo, Patrice Lumumba, in 1961; and the Korean War. A society that tolerates violence toward people of color shouldn't be surprised, Malcolm believed, that it would spiral out of control and eventually affect white people too.

Muhammad was enraged by Malcolm's editorializing, even if it was the truth, for it put a spotlight on the NOI and gave it bad press, threatening its longevity. But this was just one more conflict in their increasingly strained relationship. After taking his hajj to Mecca in Saudi Arabia and visiting the African continent in 1964, Malcolm could no longer turn a blind eye to the NOI leader's misogyny and extramarital relationships with young women, and he saw the limits of Muhammad's teachings in contrast to the untapped possibilities of pan-African solidarity and global human rights.

By the spring of 1964, Malcolm's break with Muhammad was complete. If you attended Malcolm's speeches after this time, you wouldn't hear him talk of "white devils." You would, instead, hear him say that he now welcomed white allies in the struggle; that black small business growth and entrepreneurialism promoted by the NOI wasn't a viable answer to oppression; that black pride meant little in the face of crippling poverty across the world; that blackness was a global, not only an American, experience. As Malcolm put it in an interview in the *Egyptian Gazette* in 1964, "How can we get the unity of the Afro-American community? . . . We need more light about each other. Light creates understanding, understanding creates love, love creates patience, and patience creates unity . . . We want freedom, justice, and equality, we want recognition and respect as *human beings*."[47]

Malcolm brought this civic radical message to the streets. He organized the Organization for Afro-American Unity (OAAU), whose purpose, he told several hundred people during the group's inaugural meeting in the Audubon Ballroom in Harlem on June 28, 1964, was to do for black people what King's Poor People's Campaign meant to do for everyone. Malcolm facilitated rent strikes in Harlem against decrepit living conditions imposed by landlords and proposed developing social services that weren't provided by the state. "We must establish a clinic, whereby one can get aid and cure for drug addiction," he declared. "We must set up a guardian system that will help our youth who get into trouble."[48]

Malcolm's thought is important today for a reason that might be surprising, because his ideas have been distorted for decades in popular culture. Even during his NOI years, he wasn't a virulent antiwhite racist who wanted to kill as many white people as possible, driven by a seething hatred. Malcolm matters today because of his radical love for black people: He spoke courageously and unapologetically to his own community so they would rally for themselves and resist white supremacy, which they had had no hand in creating but couldn't easily escape. He never questioned black humanity and didn't equivocate when he demanded "Freedom now!" Baldwin knew that it was because of Malcolm's unconditional love for them that black people saw him as their prophet. The black Hollywood actor Ossie Davis famously eulogized Malcolm as a "black shining Prince!" Words like Davis's, Baldwin explains in his extended essay *No Name on the Street* (1972), had to do with Malcolm's "love for blacks" and his conviction that black people can, on their own, "see their condition and change it themselves."[49]

Malcolm met Martin Luther King Jr. only once, on March 26, 1964, at the US Senate, as it was debating the passage of the 1964 Civil Rights Act. In spite of the earlier divergences in their approaches to anti-racism, their positions had fused by the end of their lives when it came to socioeconomic justice. In February 1965, holding a rally during SCLC's activities in Selma, Alabama, Malcolm personally apologized to King's wife, Coretta Scott, for not visiting Martin, who was in jail for leading a march to Selma's courthouse. "I didn't come to Selma to make his job difficult," he confided. "I really did come thinking that I could make it easier. If the white people realize what the alternative is, perhaps they will be more willing to hear Dr. King."[50] Just weeks later, the bullet of a disgruntled NOI assassin pierced Malcolm's flesh and killed him on February 21,

1965, in the very same Audubon ballroom where he had announced his new transformative vision.

James Baldwin was grief-stricken when he learned of the assassination of Malcolm X. The lovelessness that had haunted Baldwin his whole life had crescendoed with a vengeance. And three years later, Baldwin would see it again in full force. Everything fell apart when Martin Luther King Jr. was gunned down at the Lorraine Motel in Memphis on April 4, 1968, while rallying striking sanitation workers. What followed were black uprisings in Chicago, Kansas City, New York, Pittsburgh, and Detroit. When all was said and done, these tremors reached a total of 125 cities over the next week. This, in truth, was to be expected. Black America was again clearly feeling pain. No one knew it at the time, but things would just get worse.

Seven months later, in November of that year, Republican Richard Nixon was elected on a law-and-order platform—a promise to stomp out black rebellion. Over the next few decades, racial equality initiatives were either treated with benign neglect or chipped away. Few white people heeded Baldwin's, King's, and Malcolm's pleas to lead with love.

Until Baldwin died in France from stomach cancer on December 1, 1987, he was often absent from US public life when those he might inspire needed him most. As the antiblack reaction to the civil rights movement was on the rise, he spent years in Turkey and France meeting with friends and working on essays and unfinished plays. The artist overtook the activist, but his message lived on. The young black feminists, gay activists, and socialists who found guidance in his essays knew they would take up the fight against patriarchy, homophobia, racial injustice, and poverty with or without his physical presence. This is the truth of civic radicalism. It remains alive only because those who don't play by civility's rules of respectability take it up. A pressing ambition is at the forefront of their minds: a world to win.

Chapter 5

CIVIC RADICALS BELIEVE RACISM IS STRUCTURAL RATHER THAN PERSONAL

On November 19, 1970, James Baldwin wrote an open letter to the *New York Review of Books* in an effort to vividly denounce American empire. The war machine was raging in Vietnam. Politicians were vowing to stomp out the revolutionary atmosphere of the '60s. Unarmed black people were still being shot by police. Debilitating poverty was as real as ever before. Baldwin was enraged by widespread moral apathy, and he chastised the catastrophic way in which white people continued to take "refuge in whiteness." "They will perish," Baldwin prophesized in his open letter, "in their delusions."[1]

But Baldwin's cry, by turns searching and searing, seemed to be directed into the abyss. Things had changed drastically since the beginning of the civil rights movement. He was no longer trying to inspire a multiracial movement capable of reconstructing American democracy. Instead, he was mining the depths of his own despair for some grain of hope. Malcolm, Martin, Evers, and Hansberry were all dead. The rancor and suspicion between SNCC, SCLC, the NAACP, and the Black Power movement were as pronounced as ever. Two Black Panthers, Fred

Hampton and Mark Clark, were shot at point-blank range in a home raid in 1969 by the Chicago Police Department. The black freedom struggle was on life support.

America was in the throes of a far-right backlash. And the new regime in Washington was led by Republican president Richard Nixon, who had been elected in 1968 using the "Southern Strategy." Nixon's promise of restoring law and order to US cities was, in truth, a coded way to say that he would protect scared white people from the urban black menace. To get elected, he knew he needed to bring into his coalition embittered white voters who would never again vote Democrat after Johnson had betrayed them and signed civil rights legislation in the 1960s. Many of them flirted with supporting the third-party candidate, Alabama governor George Wallace, who had built his name as a segregationist. These are the voters Nixon spoke to in his "Silent Majority" speech, in which he identified what he saw as the forgotten white Americans who were entirely uninterested in political protest, social change, or racial justice—and many of whom were angered by the past decade of black protest movements. Accepting the Republican Party nomination for president on August 8, 1968, Nixon said, "It is the voice of the great majority of Americans . . . the non-shouters; the non-demonstrators. They are not racists or sick . . . They are black and they are white . . . We cannot have progress without order, we cannot have order without progress."[2]

Three out of ten white voters who had voted for Johnson in 1964 went on to vote for Nixon or Wallace in 1968. Throughout his presidency, Nixon tried to make good on his promise to them. He unsuccessfully attempted to eviscerate Section 5 of the Voting Rights Act, which required Southern states to get federal preclearance before implementing any changes to voting law. And he directed political appointees to do whatever was in their power to avoid enforcing the Supreme Court's desegregation decision in *Brown*, raising the idea of administrative obstacles and pointing to different priorities. Capitalizing on the court's famous opinion that integration proceed "with all deliberate speed," Nixon delayed and delayed, over and over again.[3]

Baldwin's letter in the *NYRB* was a warning of the oncoming disaster of renewed right-wing ascendance and liberal retreat. But, as its title—"An Open Letter to My Sister, Miss Angela Davis"—signaled, it was also part of a broader international grassroots campaign to free Davis, the black feminist and Black Panther, from prison. Born in Birmingham, Alabama, in 1944, Davis became a philosophy professor at the University of California, Los Angeles, at twenty-six, an appointment that reflected her brilliance. She was fired in 1969 by then-governor Ronald Reagan's California Board of Regents for her affiliation with the Communist Party and its youth branch, the Che-Lumumba Club. A year later, Davis was accused of purchasing the handgun that had been used by seventeen-year-old Jonathan Jackson to free his older brother, George, one of the three "Soledad Brothers" who—despite conflicting reports and evidence suggesting otherwise—had been charged with the murder of a white prison guard in Soledad Prison in California.[4]

On August 7, 1970, Jonathan stormed a Marin County courthouse where the three Soledad Brothers were being tried and demanded their unconditional freedom. A shootout ensued, and both Jonathan and the presiding judge were killed. Despite having no direct role in the exchange, Davis was singled out as public enemy number one. After a weeks-long manhunt, during which she went into hiding and was placed on the FBI's Most Wanted Listed, Davis was captured. Nixon couldn't contain his elation. Overjoyed, he commended the bureau for doing a great patriotic service in capturing the "dangerous terrorist."[5] The *New York Times* editorial pages didn't rush to her defense, lamenting that Davis could have made a "significant contribution to the nation's normal political debate and to its needed processes of peaceful change" but instead "became so alienated that she finally went over to revolutionary words and perhaps even worse."[6]

A campaign ensued to win Davis's release. Intellectuals organized conferences and wrote letters, activists marched, and musicians wrote songs. Their hard work was rewarded. After being acquitted by an all-white jury in 1972, Davis became an icon of anti-racists everywhere. She lectured at colleges and organized rallies. Her best-selling 1974 *An Autobiography*, which detailed her time spent in solitary confinement, was a metaphor for the segregation of black Americans across the country.

Davis was lucky to escape the clutches of the US penal system. But not so for the more than two thousand prisoners at the Attica Correctional Facility in Attica, New York, who—around the time of Davis's trial—were plagued by malnutrition, psychological torture, harsh working conditions, inadequate healthcare, racist prison guards, brutal violations of privacy, and obscenely unsanitary cells and cafeteria. In 1971, in an effort to secure their human rights, they took over the Attica prison and held forty-two staff hostage. After four tense but productive days, it seemed as if they were on the brink of negotiating a settlement with the authorities. But New York governor Nelson Rockefeller wouldn't stand for any kind of negotiation with the prisoners, ordering a thousand heavily armed law enforcement personnel to take the prison back by force in a chaotic scene: snipers began unloading rounds, helicopters dropped tear gas, and state troopers broke through the walls. In the aftermath, thirty-nine people were dead—twenty-nine inmates and ten guards. "They did a fabulous job," Rockefeller said when he phoned President Nixon. "It really was a beautiful operation."[7]

Rockefeller went on to become the man to give teeth to Nixon's law-and-order platform on the state level. In 1973, he signed a controversial law in New York State that set a mandatory minimum sentence of fifteen years in prison for possessing or distributing heroin or cocaine. It became the precursor for a signature law of the Reagan administration, signed in 1986 with overwhelming bipartisan support: the Anti-Drug Abuse Act.

In the 1980s, drug addiction wasn't an epidemic by any stretch of the imagination. But any tough-on-crime policy was a political winner. The losers of this game were the usual suspects: black people, brown people, and poor people. Crack was a new drug, and widely and cheaply available, while cocaine was much more expensive. A mandatory five-year minimum sentence was set for possessing five grams of crack cocaine, which was prevalent in black communities. Meanwhile, possession of five hundred grams of powdered cocaine, used in predominately affluent white communities, garnered the same five-year minimum.[8] The disparity was blatant and shameless.

This new Washington consensus, known as the War on Drugs, combined with an escalating policing crisis to ensnare even more black men and women in the criminal justice system. The "broken-windows policing" theory, introduced in a 1982 *Atlantic Monthly* article by political scientists James Q. Wilson and George Kelling, was part of the problem. It eventually became the model for departments in Newark, Los Angeles, Boston, and New York. According to their theory, strictly enforcing small incivilities such as loitering, petty vandalism, sex work, and drug dealing deterred larger scale violent crimes like homicide, armed robbery, and sexual assault. By describing city life as dystopian fiction, Wilson and Kelling engaged in a sensationalized distortion: a world in which there is crippling social anxiety, shattered glass, undisciplined bodies, and minds soaked in irreverent urges. All of this was racialized. The urban community, as they put it, could soon morph into a "jungle," in which gangs of "rowdy" children would grow up to be licentious youth.[9] The right-wing criminologist and University of Pennsylvania professor John DiIulio Jr. went even further, his language eerily similar to early-twentieth-century lynch mobs, who perceived black men as sexual predators. In a 1995 *Weekly Standard* op-ed, DiIulio said the inner city was bursting with "super-predators," who emerged from homes "where unconditional love is nowhere but unmerciful abuse is common."[10]

Implicit in this punitive understanding of community revitalization was the idea that police were saviors that established a community where none existed before. Carefully ignored in Wilson and Kelling's analysis were the community activists, union and grassroots organizers, teachers, anti-poverty workers, and progressive churches who try to heal the world one neighborhood at a time. This thinking continues today. A majority of Americans view police as heroes. A 2018 Gallup survey placed the public approval number of law enforcement at a staggering 54 percent, twice that of community activists, teachers, organized labor leaders, and even medical professionals.[11] But as history shows, empowering police to neutralize incivility simply whitewashes the corporate crimes—the predatory renting and mortgage lending, the tax evasion—that go into making unfair housing policy and that occur under the cloak of civility. It circumvents the political choices that generate poverty and that perpetuate a patriarchal society that adds to the struggle of many women and queer people.

A new theory of aggressive policing in the 1980s was just one way in which progress was thwarted and racial inequality was maintained. Another was Ronald Reagan's economic policy, which was hell-bent on privatizing everything in sight and crushing the 1960s social welfare state. The ink had barely dried on the Fair Housing Act of 1968, which rendered redlining and discriminatory housing practices illegal. And people still remembered President Lyndon Johnson's Kerner Commission, which he established in 1967 to understand the source of the urban black uprisings throughout the country that year. The report contended, "White institutions created [the black ghetto], white institutions maintain it, and white society condones it."[12]

But reactionaries wanted to justify drastic cuts to government programs like Medicaid, nutritional aid, and housing assistance as soon as possible. The libertarian conservative and Manhattan Institute fellow Charles Murray, in his highly influential book *Losing Ground* (1984), claimed that the 1960s expansion of social welfare programs only exacerbated the problems they were meant to solve, making people dependent upon federal government social assistance. Tough love was the solution, as the neoconservative public policy expert Lawrence Mead, who had served in the Nixon administration, writes in his 1986 book *Beyond Entitlement*, "Those who are free of responsibility for themselves cannot be free to make their own way in society."[13]

Reactionaries wanted to downsize government, so they argued not only that such a policy was moral but that it only affected black people, leaving out the poor white people who depended upon these programs in far greater numbers. Early on, Reagan did this through turning public attention to uncivil black citizens—this time, the single mothers purported to be robbing American taxpayers blind. In his failed 1976 presidential campaign, Reagan focused on the figure of Chicago resident Linda Taylor, whom he called the "welfare queen." Ascribing this metaphor to all public assistance recipients, Reagan described how she drove a "Cadillac, used 80 names ... 30 addresses, 15 telephone numbers to collect food stamps, Social Security, veterans' benefits for four nonexistent deceased veteran husbands, as well as welfare. Her tax-free cash income alone has been running $150,000 a year."[14] Never mind that this wasn't the way most, or even a sizable number, of welfare recipients acted. This image fit perfectly with a new racial category—the so-called antisocial underclass—that had begun to appear in center-left magazines like the *New Yorker* and in non-fiction, such as Ken Auletta's 1982 book *The Underclass*.

Talk of the underclass used color-blind language—racist monikers weren't used, neither was obvious talk of white supremacy. But reading between the lines, we can detect a thinly veiled implication that the un-derclass refers to black communities. Lawrence Mead said that 70 per-cent of the underclass, which he claimed was "mostly visible in urban slum settings," was nonwhite—about six million people—and that the urban underclass was made up of "street hustlers, welfare families, drug addicts, and former mental patients."[15] A widespread belief was again re-vived: that most black people lived in a pathological culture—defined by excess, criminality, laziness, and cheating, with echoes of Daniel Patrick Moynihan's infamous 1965 report on the black family. Black disparities in wealth, employment, housing, life expectancy, graduation rates, infant mortality, and number of single-parent households were no longer envi-sioned as products of structural inequalities past and present, as they had been, briefly, during the civil rights movement. Now, these circumstances were evidence of bad character—the refusal to work hard, to take per-sonal responsibility, be independent, and instill good moral and familial values in youth.

Conservative intellectuals zealously promoted this racist reasoning in the public sphere. Former Reagan aide and Indian American writer Dinesh D'Souza, in his best-selling book *The End of Racism* (1995), ar-gues that racism is fundamentally over—save for a few bad individual racists here or there—and that the greatest danger to black progress is programs like affirmative action. His book became something of a bible for conservatives and law-and-order liberals: "Today black culture has become an obstacle," he writes, "because it prevents blacks from taking advantage of rights and opportunities that have multiplied in a new social environment." He claims that "black pathologies . . . pose a serious threat to the survival of blacks as a group as well as to the safety and integrity of the larger society."[16]

Shelby Steele, a black professor of English at San Jose State University, elevated black psychological woundedness—hurt, despair, self-doubt, low self-esteem—as the reason for the achievement gap. In doing this, Steele ignored that school districts are funded by the property taxes of the municipality they serve, so that the quality of education almost entirely depends on a district's average income. In an award-winning book, *The Content of Our Character* (1999), which is billed by the publisher as "neither 'liberal' nor 'conservative,'" Steele writes, "I think this impulse to self-segregate, to avoid whites, has to do with the way white people are received by the black anti-self . . . The anti-self, that hidden perpetrator of racist doubt, sees white people as better than black people." [17] A certain "racial vulnerability," he says, is the reason that black schoolchildren "put forth the meagerest effort and show a virtual indifference to the genuine opportunity that is education."[18]

The black linguist John McWhorter, in *Losing the Race: Self-Sabotage in Black America* (2000), added to the chorus. He argues that the biggest danger with what he called "victimology" thinking is that "because black people endure such victimhood at every turn, they cannot be held responsible for immoral or destructive actions."[19] The structural problem of racial injustice is thus retold as personal or even racial moral failings, something easily brushed aside. The pressing public question about unequal black access to political, social, and economic power morphs into a conversation about ending personal black rage and bitterness. Policy changes like expanding social welfare, desegregating public schools, or decreasing the gap between white and black wealth are completely off the table; what is necessary is more cordial interracial debate and more civility in the heart. As Ben Carson—the once esteemed neurosurgeon turned Housing and Urban Development secretary under Trump—writes in his

2015 memoir, "Most of our public fights over racism . . . could be easily re-solved if the injured party expected the best of the offender and corrected the offensive statement in a kind and rational manner . . . if we choose to react positively rather than negatively."[20]

But anti-racists know better; civility isn't the answer. In August 1980, the self-described "black, lesbian, mother, warrior, poet" Audre Lorde got into a heated exchange with James Baldwin at Hampshire College in Amherst, Massachusetts, where he was holding a visiting professorship, during a conversation arranged by *Essence* magazine. Arguably no one in the post–civil rights era was as much Baldwin's intellectual heir as Lorde. As the greatest civic radicals had before her, Lorde had an uncanny way of seeing how fearlessness with oneself and with one's allies was nonnego-tiable. For his part, Baldwin couldn't fathom how black women's strug-gles were different from black men's. He saw white supremacy as the core problem plaguing black America, without fully appreciating the different ways, when connected to patriarchy, it impacted black men and women. Lorde was exasperated by Baldwin's bewilderment. From her perspective, he must have embodied the innocence that he himself had long accused his white countrymen of hiding behind. She put it bluntly: "Okay, the cops are killing the men and the men are killing the women. I'm taking about rape. I'm talking about murder."[21]

Born ten years after Baldwin, in 1934 in New York City, which he had also called home, Lorde was a child of immigrants from Grenada. After being active in the civil rights movement in the 1960s, she left New York and was a writer in residence at Tougaloo College, a historically black liberal arts school in Mississippi. Lorde knew geographic changes and new homes were no fix for the social marginalization she had to endure daily for being black and an out lesbian. For Lorde, politics were personal. Self-love, which she never confused with narcissism, allowed her to make a home for herself in a world hell-bent on destroying her. As she writes, "If I didn't define myself for myself, I would be crunched into other peo-ple's fantasies for me and eaten alive."[22] Lorde endorsed the aspirations of all subjugated citizens: people of color, women, poor people, migrants, colonized peoples, disabled people, gay men and women. For Lorde, this was the truest reflection of love, as she wrote in her 1978 essay "The Uses of the Erotic: The Erotic as Power": "As we begin to recognize our deepest feelings, we begin to give up, of necessity, being satisfied with suffering and self-negation . . . Our acts against oppression become integral with self, motivated and empowered from within."[23]

Not long before Lorde's exchange with Baldwin, a group of radical black lesbian feminists began a series of meetings in Boston that culminated in the Combahee River Collective Statement of 1977. The students, artists, and activists who were members of the collective argued that anti-racism meant little without intersectional thinking. They publicly supported Kenneth Edelin, a black doctor arrested in Boston for manslaughter because he had performed an abortion. They stood with striking workers who demanded that construction companies hire more black construction workers to build a high school in Boston. They were especially active during the winter of 1979, when they created ten thousand pamphlets to distribute throughout the community and to the media highlighting the underreported story of twelve black women who had been murdered within miles of one another throughout Boston between January and May of 1979—some were mutilated, others dismembered, and many sexually assaulted. After their effort had increased public attention, another group organized several protests in May of that year—but the facilitators were black men who described the violence as purely a matter of racism. The collective knew better: what had happened was about class, race, gender, and sexuality. Lorde, who lived in New York City at the time, exchanged letters with one of Combahee's members, Barbara Smith, and was kept informed of their activities, and eventually agreed to read at the Fifth Black Feminist Retreat in July. The poem she read at the retreat, "Need: A Chorale for Black Woman Voices," was a eulogy for the twelve black women who had been murdered and a call to arms against patriarchy and racism, which concluded with the line repeating, "We cannot live without our lives."[24]

Through the 1980s, until she died of liver cancer at the age of fifty-eight on November 17, 1992, Lorde was a bright light for young activists, academics, and creative writers who believed in making art political and speaking fiercely about the urgency of intersectional thinking. She was a much-needed guide in a daunting political landscape. Just weeks before her death, on November 3, 1992, an event occurred that echoed the post–Civil War era, when Republicans abandoned Reconstruction in 1877 to win the US presidency at all costs. This time, the Democratic Party, the self-appointed guardian of civil rights, betrayed its loyal black constituency out of a desperate need to demonstrate its commitment to law and order by nominating for president the charismatic governor of Arkansas, Bill Clinton. Clinton took time off from his campaign in January 1992 to personally oversee the execution of a barely cognitively functional black man on death row named Ricky Ray Rector. And in the middle of his first term, Clinton signed the Violent Crime Control and Law Enforcement Act , which gave $10 billion to federal prisons and authorized the Community Oriented Policing Services office, part of the US Department of Justice, to provide local police departments the resources to hire one hundred thousand new cops.[25]

Clinton was just getting started. Not to be outdone by his right-wing opponents, Clinton, who always touted his intelligence as a Rhodes Scholar at Oxford University, loved the premise of Murray's *Losing Ground*, that welfare had a corrosive effect on poor people. As the product of a working-class family in Little Rock and a fan of McDonald's and fried chicken, Clinton talked about his firsthand understanding of the plight of the poor. From this wellspring of empathy, Clinton believed, came his knowledge that the poor needed a "hand up, not a handout." So he proudly signed the Personal Responsibility and Work Opportunity Act of 1996 in a bipartisan effort with a Republican Congress.

Looking back, some Americans might still nostalgically point to this moment as a high-water mark of compromise between Democrats and Republicans. But if this is what bipartisan compromise creates, we should all be deeply concerned. For by replacing the New Deal program Aid for Families of Dependent Children (AFDC) with Temporary Assistance for Needy Families (TANF), the government put stringent work requirements in place for anyone needing assistance securing what are widely considered human rights: food and housing. This pushed unemployed low-income people, especially mothers with young children, into the low-wage job market, which in turn created a labor surplus and gave more power to managers to hire and fire people and to dictate their working conditions. Many poor people held several jobs in order to qualify for TANF while still living below the federal poverty line. In 1997, during his second term, Clinton gave citizens something else they couldn't eat—the One America Initiative, an executive order issued after a convention of scholars across the country resulted in a guidebook of "best practices" for educators, citizens, and community leaders to use in fostering honest and open dialogue about diversity.

It was around this time that racial reconciliation became the latest theme in the ongoing liberal discourse of civility, this time to distract from their blatant retreat from racial justice. At the local level, in predominantly black cities and neighborhoods, street names were changed and statues raised to honor black leaders such as Rosa Parks, Malcolm X, and Martin Luther King Jr. The Kelly Ingram Park of Revolution and Reconciliation was built in 1992 directly across from the Birmingham Sixteenth Street Baptist Church. Museums were erected, such as the National Civil Rights Museum in Memphis. Democratic politicians universally supported these acts of commemoration at the state, local, and national level because they cost relatively little and gave the surface impression that Democrats cared about diversity. Yet, strikingly absent from the conversation about honoring the past was talk of revolutionary transformation toward real social justice in the present. There was no discussion about raising taxes on corporations or small businesses to fund public schools, themselves slowly being replaced by private charter schools in which job security for teachers was eliminated. There was no discussion of living-wage legislation, even when the economy was booming in the 1990s. By 1995, the average hourly wage was 3 percent less than what it had been in 1989, and median family incomes were 5.9 percent lower.[26] Generally ignored during this time of economic plenty was any attempt to build community centers for youth or create affordable healthcare and clinics for those struggling with addiction.

The same government priorities have existed from that time to this day. Just days before Trump's inauguration, one of the largest philanthropic organizations in the US, the W. K. Kellogg Foundation, founded in 1930 with the fortune of the breakfast cereal creator Will Kellogg, held its first annual day of "racial healing," on January 17, 2017. The foundation devised a handbook to be used by communities across the US to talk about race—harking back to the empty reconciliation gestures of the post–Civil War era and Clinton's One America Initiative. Placing "healing" above political consciousness allowed the leaders of the Kellogg Foundation to proudly tout Trump's support for the event without acknowledging the contradictions between the event goals and Trump's campaign promises, such as Trump's demand to eliminate Obama-era rules known as "consent decrees" that required local police departments known for police brutality to institute a legal framework for reform and his desire to expand prison privatization. Just a week before the Kellogg event, however, a *Guardian* report found that black men ages fifteen to thirty-four were nine times more likely than other Americans to be killed by police—a total of 266 black men and women in 2016 alone.[27] Almost five hundred thousand black citizens are languishing behind bars, many of whom are stuck in solitary confinement, and others are on parole. To put this number in perspective, one out of eleven black citizens are under correctional control.

Another way the idea of racial reconciliation became mainstreamed over the last several decades was through public apologies. Ironically, apologies became remarkably effective not at grappling with the legacy of slavery and Jim Crow but for promoting US nationalism. Congress's official apology for slavery in 2008, 143 years after the practice was abolished by the Thirteenth Amendment, called for "a dialogue where people will open their hearts and their minds to the problems that face this country." The apology was meant to redeem the idea of historical progress and American exceptionalism, to form "a more perfect union."[28] More shockingly, the US Senate's 2005 resolution apologizing for federal inaction against lynching sought to purify America's status abroad as the Bush administration was waging a war on people of color that would, after more than a decade, result in over six hundred thousand Iraqi and Afghan civilian deaths, the price for democratic peace in both countries. The resolution stated, "Only by coming to terms with history can the United

States effectively champion human rights abroad."[29] Black pain was summoned to cement moral American militarism on foreign soil, while the government denied the ongoing disaster of human rights at home.

While liberals were asking for forgiveness for the crimes of the past, Republicans were rebranding themselves. The compassionate conservatism of the early 2000s was a modern invocation of slaveholder civility. Many Americans now recall George W. Bush's leadership from 2001 to 2009 fondly and might even pine for his approach as a relic of a gentler, purer, and more tolerant era. But here is what he, a man whose political rise was based on redemption as a born-again evangelical Christian who renounced his youthful drug use, alcoholism, draft-dodging, and poor academic performance at Yale, said two years after his election in 2002: "Compassionate conservatism offers a new vision for fighting poverty in America . . . For millions of younger Americans, welfare became a static and destructive way of life."[30]

Bush's administration displayed the opposite of compassion, namely apathy, when Hurricane Katrina hit New Orleans in September 2005. Black citizens drowned in flooded streets and died of thirst due to lack of clean drinking water. Seventy percent of homes were damaged, two thousand deaths were recorded (and more were unaccounted for), and relief shelters housed around 270,000 people. In the aftermath of the disaster, Bush enlisted compassionate conservatism to make the ruins of what Mayor Ray Nagin referred to as the "chocolate city" a safe haven for the real estate industry, charter schools, and oil companies. "In New Orleans and in other places," Bush said, "many of our fellow citizens have felt excluded from the promise of our country. The answer is not only temporary relief, but schools that teach every child, and job skills that bring upward mobility, and more opportunities to own a home and start a business."[31] What transpired were gentrifying neighborhoods in which black people couldn't afford to live, black neighborhoods in which homes were never rebuilt, and low paying jobs, when jobs existed at all.

In the years since, little has changed. In a 2017 town hall debate, Republican Speaker of the House, Wisconsin representative Paul Ryan, said he saw no contradiction between, on one hand, speaking of his loving

Catholic convictions and, on the other hand, in arguing for cutting taxes for the wealthy; rolling back regulations for corporations; and privatizing Social Security and Medicare, programs that working people depend on. As he explained, "The poor are being marginalized and misaligned in many ways because a lot of the programs that we have, well intended as they may be, are discouraging and dis-incentivizing work."[32]

But civic radicals weren't silent during this concerted effort by politicians on the right and the left to con the American public. Three years after Clinton signed his crime bill and one year after the evisceration of welfare, in 1997, Angela Davis founded Critical Resistance, the prison abolitionist network, at a conference in Berkeley, California. Thousands of activists, artists, filmmakers, novelists, students, ex-prisoners, and policymakers attended the three-day event that included over two hundred panels. Its purpose was to brainstorm how to confront the mass incarceration crisis, which had become a problem of unprecedented proportions, with especially disastrous consequences for people of color. Critical Resistance chapters were organized in Portland, Oakland, New York, and Los Angeles.

The movement never received significant mainstream coverage, but in op-eds, essays, and academic monographs, the self-described "new abolitionists" would educate us that prisons weren't natural responses to increased crime but a new way to punish black people and manage broader socioeconomic crises. In her groundbreaking book *Golden Gulag* (2007), the critical geographer Ruth Wilson Gilmore interpreted the growing prison population in the state of California as a spatial, political, and economic nexus through which the state confronted deindustrialization, which happened when big businesses, looking for cheaper labor around the globe and investing more capital in automation, shuttered their factories and fled American cities. Black prisoners were housed in prisons in primarily white rural areas, which created jobs in the local community and depressed black political mobilization in major cities. These prisons employed workers laid off from military manufacturing plants that had closed in the 1960s, and the number of black people able to vote and organize to challenge prison expansion exponentially decreased.

Prison abolitionists raised the alarm about the deadening effects of what they called the "prison industrial complex" on democracy. Prisons, they said, would become schools for reproducing society's toxic masculinity, ruthless competition, and petty self-interest. Solitary confinement would foster social alienation. Voter disenfranchisement for felony conviction would weaken political opposition. In relation, schools would be more militarized, with metal detectors, police raids, armed security guards, and active-shooter drills becoming essential to the experience of education. After twenty years and counting, many of these predictions have been borne out.

Critical Resistance brought this knowledge to the grassroots level. For example, as part of its Leadership, Education, Action, and Dialogue Project (LEAD), founded in 2004, incarcerated women of color in LA— whose numbers had increased by 800 percent since the 1980s as the result of the prosecution of small-scale drug offenses—were organized through workshops and training exercises to investigate oppressive processes. They soon became aware that the sexist society in which they lived on the outside would be reproduced on the inside by placing incarcerated women under surveillance and at greater risk for sexual violence by male guards. More recent pressure campaigns have included opposition to LA's increased jail construction—especially so-called mental health jails—and protest against the annual Urban Shield police training program, funded by the Department of Homeland Security, which, since 2007, had invited law enforcement officials to an expo at the Alameda County Fairgrounds to train with the latest high-tech military-grade weaponry. After years of relentless agitation led by Critical Resistance, in March 2019, Urban Shield finally shut down.

This is what new abolitionists propose: disarming and ultimately defunding police; promoting community solutions rather than punitive measures in schools; implementing restorative justice initiatives based in interpersonal mediation between perpetrators and victims; increasing wages for poor people; providing more affordable housing and greater mental health access; decriminalizing drugs and sex work and ending sexual assault. Beyond the ambitious goal of shuttering prisons entirely, the immediate pragmatic concerns of abolitionists center on urging legislatures to pass shorter sentences for felony convictions, unionizing prison labor, and creating better connections between those on the inside and the outside. "The creation of new institutions that lay claim to the space now occupied by the prison," Davis writes in her 2003 book *Are Prisons Obsolete?*, "can eventually start to crowd out the prison so that it would inhabit increasingly smaller areas of our social and psychic landscape."[33]

As prison abolitionists were out in the streets touting their unflinching realism and clear-eyed assessment of the dynamics of power, there was a faint sense of hope that things might be different with the 2008 presidential campaign of Barack Obama. But abolitionists and other activists were sorely disappointed. The Harvard Law graduate—icon of racial integration and post-racialism, son of a white Kansan mother and a black Kenyan father—boasted of his progressive credentials as a former community organizer on Chicago's South Side. But in the same breath, he rehashed the time-honored talking points on racial reconciliation that had been perfected by Bush, Clinton, and Reagan before him, so as not to be seen as being too easy on his fellow black citizens. Obama, whose own father left the family when Obama was young, sometimes described black men as the agents of black community disrepair. What wasn't front and center in Obama's speeches was the fact that black men were stopped and frisked by police at exceedingly high rates and viewed as a clear and present danger when simply walking down the street or driving their cars. Instead, Obama said, during a Father's Day speech at a majority-black church, "Too many fathers . . . are missing. . . . They have abandoned their responsibilities, acting like boys instead of men. And the foundations of our families are weaker because of it. . . . And the foundations of our community are weaker because of it."[34]

Well into his second term, Obama would continue to use this scolding tone, especially in his response to the 2015 demonstrations in Baltimore after a twenty-five-year-old black man, Freddie Gray, had his spine dislocated while in police custody. Gray later died, and Obama juxtaposed legitimate civil protests that flared up in the city against police brutality with "a handful of criminals and thugs who tore up the place." Obama was dismayed by the fact that the peaceful protest did not get as much attention as the "senseless violence and destruction" that occurred. "That is not a protest," he said. "It is not a statement. It's people—a handful of people, taking advantage of a situation for their own purposes, and they need to be treated as criminals."[35] And yet, Obama focused on the violent aspects of the protest himself, only to demonize it. The dichotomy between good and evil, or civil and uncivil, was at work again here. The mayor of Baltimore at the time, Stephanie Rawlings-Blake, who is black, doubled down: "It is very clear the difference between what we saw, over the past week with the peaceful protests, those who wish to seek justice, those who wish to be heard and want answers, and the difference between those protests and the thugs."[36]

It is possible that Obama used the word "thug" in an attempt to venerate the nonviolent protests in Baltimore. And it is possible that Rawlings-Blake used the word in the heat of the moment. But these influential leaders' insistence that their comments were color-blind—and even Obama's unwillingness to rescind his comment, even after widespread rebuke— is betrayed by the racist meaning that word has acquired. The word is soaked in a history that was unleashed by their comments in ways they may or may not have sanctioned or ever expected.

During Obama's presidency, violence against unarmed black citizens was given public visibility like never before. Perpetrators justified their attacks by claiming to have been confronting uncivil civilians who needed to be contained and disciplined. In 2014, an eighteen-year-old black teen, Michael Brown was fatally shot by white police officer Darren Wilson in Ferguson, Missouri. Wilson later stated that he saw Brown as a "demon," a "Hulk Hogan," almost superhuman, invincible. Brown appeared too unruly as he walked toward and then away from Wilson's car, with his hands up. A young black woman, Renisha McBride, was killed just outside Detroit in 2013 because she came to a white neighbor's door at night asking for directions. A twelve-year-old black boy, Tamir Rice, was shot by police in 2014 in Cleveland because he was carrying a toy pistol next to a playground. A fifty-year-old black veteran, Walter Scott, was shot by a white police officer, Michael Slager, while fleeing on foot after a traffic stop for a broken brake light in North Charleston, South Carolina, in 2015.

One might think that all these events would have elicited universal outrage. But the opposite happened: predominately black people were outraged, and when they expressed their anger, they were, if not dismissed completely, treated with disdain. Law enforcement officials and defense attorneys who defended the white perpetrators rushed to marshal evidence of the black victims' illegal deeds, as if to imply that they had had it coming. Michael Brown was smoking marijuana; Walter Scott had lapsed child support payments; Renisha McBride had a high blood alcohol level. These people were killed, the popular argument went, because they were criminals. Criminality was a character trait that could be used to explain all black behavior at all times. It was the mitigating evidence that exonerated killing in cold blood.

The characterization of black people as criminals continued, unsurprisingly, in court. The key witness for the prosecution in the Trayvon Martin murder trial, a nineteen-year-old black woman named Rachel Jeantel, who was the last person the victim spoke to before he was killed, was treated as if she were on trial herself. She was depicted by the *American Conservative* writer Rod Dreher in 2013 as an illiterate, carefree alcoholic. Dreher pointed to Jeantel's misspelled social media posts and her statement that the social media backlash against her testimony made her want to drink. "Have you seen the government's star witness?" Dreher asked. "She's no Hannah Arendt."[37] In Dorian Johnson, the key black witness to the shooting of Michael Brown, Dreher saw a "jailbird" whom he criticized for "[remaining] with Big Mike [Michael Brown] after watching Big Mike steal cigarillos. Trouble follows troublemakers. Stay away from them."[38]

This response explains why the public commentary during the Ferguson protests that erupted after Michael Brown's death in 2014 was largely fixated on isolated acts of looting and arson that occurred rather than the systemic racism that had led to these acts of desperation and opportunism. Missing from the discussion was the fact that the Ferguson police department—like many across the country—had come to function as a clandestine tax collection agency used to replenish the defunded city, which had suffered for years under austerity measures brought on by tax cuts, privatization, and deregulation, which emptied the public coffers. In 2013 alone, the year before Brown was shot, Ferguson's court issued 32,975 arrest warrants in a city of 21,135 people, in a city in which a majority-white police force imposed millions of dollars of traffic fines on a majority-black city. Police officers were deployed to collect revenue for city expenditures, and doing so provided a rationale for them to keep their jobs. With such a policy in place, it made sense for police officers to aggressively write tickets and make as many arrests as possible.[39]

Within this cultural context, a new rallying cry rose up, one that combined the insights of black feminism and prison abolition: Black Lives Matter. Founded in 2012 on a Twitter hashtag by three queer black women—Alicia Garza, Patrisse Cullors, and Opal Tometi—Black Lives Matter was their response to the murder of Trayvon Martin. In the years since, the hashtag has become a movement whose overarching objective is to end police brutality. BLM activists correctly argue that over-policing in black and brown communities is a symptom of structural racism. In a society in which whiteness is still the norm and in which only white people are truly free to enjoy public space, Black Lives Matter points out, whites can summon police with startling ease, whether to inspect the legitimacy of a black Yale graduate student studying for exams (May 2018); black men gathering at Starbucks in Philadelphia (April 2018); or black families barbecuing at a public park in Oakland (May 2018). These calls to police are always framed as a matter of safety.

As long as American society celebrates the twin ideals of self-defense and white supremacy, white people will deputize themselves as legitimate wardens of civil society. A "stand your ground" law—which supports citizens' right to defend themselves, using deadly force if necessary, rather than call the police—was the basis of George Zimmerman's defense for killing Trayvon Martin. As he followed Martin, he told the local 911 dispatcher, "These assholes always get away."[40] In 2012, the same year Martin was killed, there was a dispute about loud music playing from an SUV at a gas station in Jacksonville, Florida. A white man, Michael Dunn, told

Jordan Davis, a black teen sitting in the SUV, "You're not gonna talk to me like that!" before firing multiple shots through the car and killing Davis.[41]

Black Lives Matter activists also remind us to abandon the focus on "black-on-black crime," an issue that began to receive national attention in the 1980s, when the *Chicago Tribune* ran a multi-segment story on Chicago youth violence.[42] The discussion of black-on-black crime distracts from systemic racism and distorts cause and effect. The reason a crime committed by a black person is likely to affect other black people (the same, by the way, is true for white people) is entirely explained by de facto nationwide racial segregation. Few people in the US live in truly integrated communities. Such segregation isn't produced by bad personal choices but by racist housing policies, including redlining and discriminatory mortgage lending, which have been entrenched in American culture for almost a hundred years.

From the beginning, Black Lives Matter was met with outrage from the political right. The leading proponent of broken-windows policing, former New York mayor Rudy Giuliani, said on Fox News in June 2016, "If they meant 'Black Lives Matter,' they would be doing something about the way in which the vast majority of blacks are killed in America, which is by other blacks."[43] There is a thin line between Giuliani's comments and the claims of James Comey, the former FBI director who has been embraced by the bipartisan Resistance as the civil antithesis to Trump. In 2015, Comey attributed a spike in crime in Baltimore not to expected fluctuations based on years of data, but rather to the "Ferguson effect"—the theory that requiring police accountability is itself a threat to public safety. According to Comey, police officers have told him that body cameras, viral videos, and citizen bystanders are part of the problem. Officers no longer want to engage with citizens when they might otherwise have. "We're not doing that so much anymore," the officers reportedly said to Comey, "because we don't feel like being that guy in the video."[44] This unwillingness to hold police officers accountable for their actions is expressed in Manhattan Institute scholar Heather Mac Donald's assertion that "there is no government agency more dedicated to the proposition that black lives matter more than the police . . . When the police refrain from pro-active policing, black lives are lost."[45] For Mac Donald, any check on police power is unacceptable: if you protest, police will abandon your city.

This backlash to Black Lives Matter only intensified when the slogan "Blue Lives Matter" was coined by law enforcement in December 2014, after the homicide of two NYPD police officers, Rafael Ramos and Wenjian Lu, by Ismaaiyl Brinsley—allegedly in retaliation for the death of Michael Brown. The idea behind Blue Lives Matter, which is framed as a direct response to Black Lives Matter, is that police work is most strenuous in the most dangerous (read black) neighborhoods and that it needs to be treated with more respect. At this point, what had once been a right-wing talking point morphed into a legislative initiative. In 2017 alone, as many as thirty-two state legislatures introduced Blue Lives Matter bills to put crimes against police in the same category as hate crimes against black, gay, and disabled people; women; and religious minorities.[46]

The liberal response to this development has been toothless. In their rush to be civil—to respect both sides of the divide—many liberals presume that most police work is heroic, and, even worse, they mistakenly confuse it with a real, immutable identity. *New York Times* columnist Nicholas Kristof points out, "Most of us understand that police officers are often in an impossible position, and we appreciate their courage and good work. . . . Some on the left who are aghast at racial profiling are sometimes prone to career profiling: We should stereotype neither black youths nor white cops."[47]

As the Blue Lives versus Black Lives debate was raging, the country was in the midst of a right-wing insurgency reminiscent of the worst days of the post-Reconstruction era—except this time, it wasn't just in the South but throughout the country. Beginning roughly around the time Obama was elected in 2008, Republican state legislatures and governors in places including North Carolina, Ohio, Wisconsin, and Texas began to weaponize the law to disenfranchise communities of color with startling precision. Citizens of color tend to vote Democratic. And it wasn't enough for Republicans that, in many states, citizens—many of them black—who have been convicted of a felony would be permanently disenfranchised. So they passed restrictive voter identification laws, closed polling places in majority black counties, limited absentee voting, and abolished same-day registration. Georgia's egregious "use it or lose it" law purged 107,000 citizens from the voter rolls in 2017 who hadn't voted in recent elections.[48]

To justify this antidemocratic policy, Republicans invoked the specters of deficient civic responsibility and voter fraud. In a 2011 op-ed, a leading figure in the right-wing movement and founder of True the Vote, Hans von Spakovsky, contributed to false conspiracy theories when he wrote, "A 2010 election in Missouri that ended in a one-vote margin of victory included 50 votes cast illegally by citizens of Somalia." A judge had ruled that there was no election fraud in the case, a fact that von Spakovsky failed to mention in his editorial.[49] Underlying the right's demonstrably false concern about empirically nonexistent voter fraud is their claim that requiring voter IDs and keeping addresses on the voter rolls current at all times is a small price to pay to ensure what they call, in their Orwellian tongue, "election integrity."

The libertarian law professor Ilya Somin says that because political ignorance is so widespread, it makes sense for citizens to turn their attention away from the voting booth and to "foot voting." As he writes, "If healthcare and education policy were controlled at the state or local level, or by the private sector, we would have many options to choose from, by voting with our feet. And those choices are likely to be better-informed than ballot-box decisions about the same issues are."[50] Notice how in this striking argument democracy in local contexts is conjured to encourage states' rights arguments, which have historically never been the engine for freedom but have justified slavery, segregation, union busting, and attacks on reproductive rights. If we accept this right-wing position—that democracy simply means greater personal choice—then we can dismiss voter disenfranchisement efforts as irrelevant and nonvoting as a rational, if not smart, choice. The burden falls upon citizens to prove their interest in their right to vote. This is dangerous for any democracy. But it has gained such traction in American culture that a 5–4 Supreme Court conservative majority in *Husted v. Randolph Institute* (2018) upheld as constitutional an Ohio law that canceled citizens' voter registration if, after two years of voting inactivity, they didn't respond to letters in the mail requesting confirmation of their current address.

Whether they like it or not, liberals aren't innocent in perpetuating the right's thinking about the need for marginalized citizens to be more civic-minded. A common refrain over the past few years is that Trump won in 2016 because young, old, poor, and nonwhite people were too carefree and apathetic about the importance of the election in states including Michigan, Pennsylvania, and Wisconsin. In these three states combined, Trump won roughly eighty thousand more votes than Clinton and was thus, in a winner-take-all system, awarded all forty-six electoral college votes. This swung the election in his favor even though he lost the nationwide popular vote to Clinton by almost three million votes. But calling out marginalized people for their insufficient patriotic sentiment places blame on the wrong segment of the population and distracts from the biggest single reason for Trump's win: the 92 percent of Republican voters who voted for him. These are the self-identified white moderate suburbanites, bipartisan centrists, fiscally conservative swing-voters, moral majority evangelicals, and "never Trumpers" who, after much public hand-wringing, voted for Trump anyway. And since then, many of these people have gladly reaped the benefits of the Republican agenda, which has included massive corporate tax cuts, deregulation of the oil industry and big banks, and an assault on reproductive rights.

And yet, focusing our attention on the 2016 presidential election misses what has been happening on the ground. The struggle for democracy has been ongoing despite Republican disenfranchisement efforts and Democratic chastising of the disenfranchised. On April 29, 2013, a group of seventy-five citizens came to ground zero of the Republican-led voter purges: the state legislature of North Carolina. North Carolina's governor, Pat McCrory, was trying to turn back the clock in a way that would have made the state's native son, Thomas Dixon, proud. Photo IDs were required, and many days of early voting were eliminated, as were same-day registration and out-of-precinct voting. The protesters who entered the state house on April 29 were arrested for trespassing, but they returned every week, their numbers growing with each visit. After three months, over a thousand had been jailed. The movement, which became known as Moral Mondays, had multifaceted objectives expressed by its members' literature, news statements, and media appearances. Their overriding goal was to undo North Carolina's restrictive voter ID laws and blatantly racist gerrymandering, while also raising the national alarm about environmental racism, mass incarceration, US militarization, and poverty, which afflicts forty million Americans.[51]

The leader of Moral Mondays was the Reverend William Barber, a black minister. Born on August 30, 1963, in Indianapolis to a father who was an ordained minister and a mother who was a government worker, Barber at first wanted to be a civil rights lawyer before being swayed by radical religious teachings when he was a divinity student in the master's program at Duke University. As a young seminarian, Barber devoured the work of the black liberation theologian James Cone, who preached that fighting poverty and racism was godly work, and the teachings of Reinhold Niebuhr, a theologian and professor who insisted on redeeming the fragile practice of democracy in the face of its betrayal. What moved Barber most, however, were Martin Luther King Jr.'s late-1960s sermons. Hearing King denounce corporate greed, white apathy, and US imperialism helped Barber decide to commit himself to what he called a new Poor People's Movement.

Barber is no communist like Angela Davis, and he doesn't explicitly use many of the academic concepts embraced by her or Black Lives Matter. But his work is no less revolutionary. Religious movements, like secular ones, needn't be mired in reactionary fundamentalism. The transcendent promise they describe on the horizon is what motivates believers to act with purpose and faith. Remember the force of Quakerism in the antislavery movement or the role of the black church in the assault on Jim Crow. At stake for the Poor People's Movement is the prospect of creating a new language of collective responsibility that seizes the moral terrain from right-wing evangelism, which has for decades co-opted religion for exclusionary ends through Reverend Jerry Falwell's organization, the Moral Majority. Moral revival, for Barber, means combating xenophobia, not putting undocumented people in cages. It means a living wage, not tax cuts; gender liberation, not assaults on women's reproductive freedom. Barber knows his charisma isn't the main event, and neither is his leadership. As a devotee of the democratic teachings of Ella Baker, which stress organizing alongside everyday people rather than top-down leadership, Barber turned down vocal requests to be the NAACP's national president and eventually stepped away from his directorship position of the North Carolina branch of the organization in October 2017.

The civic radical knows that microphones, loudspeakers, and podiums only do so much. Far more important is the daily grind of organizing and bearing witness. And this is what the Poor People's Movement has done over the past few years. The road ahead, as King declared half a century ago and as Barber remembers, is excruciatingly long and unimaginably treacherous. But we have nothing without hope, and time will move forward whether we like it or not. The question is whether the future will bring more of the same or a rupture that reveals something we've never seen.

This is the real question about the future: Will history relent in its avalanche of repeated injustices, or will something new emerge from the rubble, perhaps even the progressive vista we've glimpsed somewhere in the distance? "Moral movements have never known ahead of time how long we would have to struggle before we reach higher ground," Barber wrote in his 2016 call to arms, *The Third Reconstruction*. "But we've always known that, when we get there, every little thing is gonna be all right. . . . [So] we say to one another, 'Forward together! Not one step back!'"[52]

Chapter 6

CIVILITY IS DEPLOYED WHEN DEMOCRATIC MOVEMENTS ARE ON THE RISE AND REACTIONARIES ARE ON THE ROPES

Alive and well is the bipartisan call for greater civility in our public discourse, which, we are told, is more divisive than ever. A 2019 Georgetown University poll found that 88 percent of Americans are worried that "the uncivil and rude behavior of many politicians" was taking the country in a dangerous direction.[1] In an effort to ameliorate these concerns, writers have taken to the opinion pages to offer guidance regarding the norms of public conduct. Jonathan Zimmerman, professor of education at the University of Pennsylvania, writing for a local NPR affiliate in 2019, said,

> What we need are Republicans who will raise their voices when Trump ridicules an opponent, whatever the issue at hand. You can't proclaim your desire for a more decent style of discourse, then turn a deaf ear when your own president undermines it.
>
> By the same token, though, Democrats who want bipartisan unity are going to have to tone down some of the language they use against Donald J. Trump.[2]

In an April 2019 *USA Today* column, Isadora Rangel writes, "Civility can only be achieved when we look at our behavior first. If the majority of us weren't engaged on some level in uncivil behavior, then we wouldn't have the issue in the first place."[3] This is what we are told: Listen to opposing viewpoints and empathize more. Turn down the temperature. Stop being so heated. Don't be so tribal. Refrain from hurling insults. Look to compromise when you can. Such aspirational thinking might lift up the soul and move us to sing patriotic hymns about a shared American identity, inspiring us to believe we have more in common than not.

If only it were really that simple. Over the past few years, the greatest beneficiary of calls for civility has been not the progressive left but the reactionary right. Even though we may disagree with their extreme ideas, we're told to consider all viewpoints.

Many liberals worry about internalizing the same uncivil hate that they see in their conservative opponents. So ideas hostile to equality are invited into the mainstream under the guise of civility and cloaked as tenable, even if controversial, positions. Neo-Nazis, white nationalists, xenophobes, alt-righters, and anti-Semites aren't just being tolerated. They are being invited into the public sphere: in op-eds, on cable news, and on television programs.

Weeks after Trump's election in 2016, NPR correspondent Kelly McEvers talked to a leading voice of white supremacy—Richard Spencer. Spencer later became a key figure in organizing the racist march on Charlottesville, Virginia, in August 2017, where a white supremacist drove his car over and killed nonviolent anti-racist protester Heather Heyer. Pro-life groups like Students for Life of America and March for Life clamor for a seat at the annual Women's March in Washington, positioning themselves as moral citizens who believe in the sanctity of life from "the womb to the tomb." Never Trumpers—such as former leading neoconservative intellectual Bill Kristol, chief architect of and continued apologist for the US invasion of Iraq in 2003 during the George W. Bush presidency—chastise the erosion of democratic norms under Trump's presidency. But they want to reclaim US hegemony across the globe and get tough with countries including Russia, Iran, and North Korea. Nativist anti-immigrant organizations like the Center for Immigration Studies, a think tank the Southern Poverty Law Center describes as having a "decades-long history of circulating racist writers, while also associating with white nationalists,"[4] join the new bipartisan chorus calling for greater border security. Too often missing from this conversation is the fact that the issue of border security was manufactured by Ronald Reagan in the 1980s and taken up by Bill Clinton in the 1990s, after the militarization of the US-Mexico border became a way to secure Democratic votes and to create new jobs for border patrol agents in a post-industrializing economy, in which factory work was harder to find.

Leaving far-right ideas uncontested means extreme demands will define what is practical. There might not be an actual concrete border wall along the US-Mexico border, but there is already more funding for border police, surveillance technology, and fencing. Maybe the US won't have a complete shutdown of immigration—especially of Muslims— but there are already severe restrictions on refugee and migrant entry. There won't be an elimination of tax on the super rich, but neither has there been any increase in their taxes. The government might acknowledge the scientific fact of global warming, but they won't reduce carbon emissions, on the grounds that the economy would be curtailed by the monetary cost.

Furthermore, as capitalism searches for ever-new markets in the name of robust growth and job creation, civility will continue to be a refrain used to undermine working people's freedom. Even as the workforce becomes increasingly contingent, with few benefits or labor protections—in many large companies, such as Apple, Google, and Walmart, unionization is treated with disdain, and work is as deregulated as possible—corporations continue to talk about social responsibility and humanitarian concern. Start-ups fund human-interest programming on National Public Radio and create philanthropic wings to end malaria in Africa. Companies' diversity initiatives, along with financial donations to Democratic candidates, assure us that they are part of the solution to racial prejudice, but they don't raise wages for their workers. The scions of Wall Street and the big oil profiteers are now interested in co-opting the message of environmentalists. They promise, as the conservative energy lobbying firm Clearpath puts it, to bring us "clean energy" through hydraulic fracking, thereby minimizing the reliance on traditional fossil fuels.[5]

Moreover, it's wrong to believe corporations and political elites who tell us that technological changes (self-driving vehicles, advanced computer systems, algorithms) and a more flexible labor force (Uber drivers, part-time Amazon workers, and seasonal employees who can work multiple jobs and choose their own hours) will revolutionize society. These changes benefit only capitalists and elected officials chasing not votes but money. And unless we overturn the system of profit-maximization and the political nihilism of our government representatives, these changes will simply allow for continued exploitation of the workforce. Challenging these conditions through the labor movement will be increasingly difficult after the Supreme Court decision in *Janus v. AFSCME* (2018), in which a 5–4 conservative majority overruled almost forty-one years of precedent since *Abood v. Detroit Board of Education* (1977), which allowed unions to collect fees from all workers who benefitted from the contracts they negotiated. In *Janus*, the court said that required union dues—the lifeblood of a successful and vibrant organization—are unconstitutional under the First Amendment.

Whatever the future holds, one thing that has been true historically is also true today: civility is deployed as democratic movements are ascending and reactionaries are on the ropes. While Trump won the electoral college, he lost the popular vote by three million. And none of Trump's signature policy initiatives has received anywhere close to majority support among the public. Think, for instance, of Trump's proposed border wall, his child separation policy at the US-Mexico border, his call for a Muslim immigration ban, and his tax cuts for corporations. It's true that Trump's instincts are authoritarian, evident in his desire to muzzle the press, demonize political opponents, unlawfully circumvent Congress, and suppress protest and dissent whenever possible through Twitter tirades and executive orders. This tendency is also apparent in the action for which he was impeached by the House of Representatives in January 2020: withholding $400 million in military aid to Ukraine, an ally nation, until it opened an investigation into his assumed Democratic political rival in the 2020 election, former vice president Joe Biden.

But closer inspection reveals that, ultimately, Trump's presidency is not a political movement by which he is trying to win over the hearts and minds of American citizens and cement a formidable ideological legacy. Rather, Trump's actions reveal his true goals: to leverage political power to plunder as much as possible from the public trust without getting caught. These goals are the real problem with his presidency, not his uncivil behavior. His administration's objectives include theft and the hoarding of resources for the sake of petty self-enrichment, as well as the creation of a patronage system that benefits friends—lobbyists, aides, and administration officials who come and go through a revolving door at the White House.

So when we hear Trump talking about his unrivaled greatness and touting his strong man credentials, we should know that these claims are meant to distract from his weak political authority. More often than not, the more politicians publicly tout policies to crack down on incivility, the more vulnerable they are. Real power that has a robust administrative apparatus and overwhelming popular support doesn't need to flaunt itself through displays that easily generate backlash and mass discontent. Trump's petty brutality through executive orders is despicable: Ripping asylum-seeking children from their parents at the border and imprisoning them in detention camps. Creating a Muslim ban, supposedly for the sake of national security. But his approval rating stands at an average of 42 percent. This is far different from George W. Bush's ability to galvanize virtually the entire Senate and a vast majority of the House to support the Patriot Act weeks after 9/11, and, eventually, unleash a war in Iraq in 2003 that initially enjoyed 71 percent approval.

Bipartisan patriotism enabled Bush's policies. But Trump's policies are fought at every turn, defiantly met with Black Lives Matter, #MeToo, Fight for 15, Dakota Access Pipeline protests, and strikes by teachers across the country in places like Oklahoma, West Virginia, Arizona, and Los Angeles. The media is fixated on Trump's chaotic White House and his uncivil tongue, and they report his every word on the social media platform Twitter. But much more instructive are the responses of these burgeoning liberation movements whose leaders aren't afraid to directly oppose him and the conservative ideology the Republican Party stands for. And why should they be?

Democratic socialists clamor for universal healthcare and a living wage. Feminists want to overturn patriarchy in all areas of life rather than simply educating "bad apple" misogynists. Queer activists rethink the cultural presumption that heterosexuality is normal and don't simply settle for the right to get married. Environmentalists go beyond carbon credits and see as essential the elimination of the fossil fuel industry and the creation of good jobs in renewable energy. Undocumented rights activists want to abolish Immigration and Customs Enforcement (ICE), which was only formed fifteen years ago in the wake of 9/11, under the Department of Homeland Security.

A bright future exists for these activists, many of whom are young people becoming directly engaged for the first time in a fight for a better world on a scale that we haven't seen since the 1960s. But the reactionary response is already underway. Alexandria Ocasio-Cortez, a democratic socialist elected to the House in 2018, is told to cease and desist in her talk of funding a Green New Deal by a 70 percent tax rate on the 1 percent. One GOP lawmaker, Utah Republican Rob Bishop, was so upset by Ocasio-Cortez's plan that in March 2019 he hyperbolically described it as "tantamount to genocide" for rural America.[6] Similarly, newly emboldened anti–political correctness liberals have found common ground with old-school misogynists arguing that the #MeToo movement, after only beginning to bring to the fore the way millions of women are sexually assaulted on a daily basis, has already led to "reverse sexism" and ruined the lives of many innocent men. The *New York* magazine writer Andrew Sullivan describes #MeToo in the following way: "Any presumption of innocence was regarded as a misogynist dodge . . . The righteous exposure of hideous abuse of power . . . morphed into a more generalized revolution against the patriarchy."[7]

Anti-racist protesters on college campuses are labeled as uncivil totalitarian anti-pluralist monsters wallowing in their privileged status as special snowflakes. All because they dare to protest when white nationalists are invited to give lectures for exorbitant fees paid through tuition dollars. The essayist Jonathan Chait described this student activism in April 2017 as part of the growing "illiberal left," which "has used the fear of Donald Trump to goad broader elements of the progressive movement to adopt their repressive methods and slogans. The slogan 'shut it down!' has come into fashion on the left . . . The illiberal left has brought its notion that opposing views can and should be shut down into wide circulation."[8]

Republicans have their own axe to grind regarding what they deem uncivil progressives. If you listen to them, you would think it's the uncivil activists and not the racists who are the real threat to democracy. In her 2018 Senate election bid, Cindy Hyde-Smith, a white senator from Mississippi—the state with the most brutal history of lynching in the South—ran against a black Democrat, Mike Espy. Hyde-Smith said she was just joking when, at a campaign event, she said of a white supporter that she loved him so much that "if he invited me to a public hanging, I'd be on the front row." Some US media outlets didn't ascribe intention to Hyde-Smith's words, giving credence to the senator's claim that her comment had nothing to do with race. They described it as "racially controversial" or "racially charged" rather than connecting her words to the long history—from Nixon's Southern Strategy to Reagan's welfare queen to George H. W. Bush's Willie Horton political ad in 1988 to Trump's birther myth—of pandering to the element of the white electorate consumed by racial resentment.[9] Within hours, Hyde-Smith had weaponized civility to turn the tables on anti-racists. When she declared that her own words had been "twisted . . . as a weapon against me," she effectively displaced responsibility onto the troublemakers who had dared to speak up.[10] Hyde-Smith knew what she was doing, going on to win her Senate race by over 7 percent.

The only way for civic radicals to successfully counter the civility zeitgeist is by changing the entire vocabulary of contemporary politics. We have to be wary of criminal justice reform tethered to national security. The newest wave of federal criminal justice reform, the FIRST STEP Act, passed in 2018, is based on reducing mandatory minimum sentences, which have spiraled out of control over the past thirty years. But the act does nothing to change the school-to-prison pipeline or address the lack of access to healthcare for addiction and mental illness that leads to unstable and unsheltered populations, which are then policed and jailed. What FIRST STEP does, however, is optimize a fresh pool of cheap and insecure labor for the benefit of corporations. Unsurprisingly, one of the act's key sponsors is the Koch Industries libertarian lobbying wing, Freedom Partners, whose zealous defense of free markets is only matched by its hostility toward a living wage and unions. Under FIRST STEP, rather than languishing behind bars, prisoners have the chance to earn early release and then are funneled into precarious low-wage work. FIRST STEP implements algorithms and big data to determine who can cash in for "time-earned" credits for good behavior and thus be released early. But the data used by this program is hardly objective, and it only reinforces already existing racist ideas about who is likely to engage in recidivism. Even more troubling, FIRST STEP intensifies the reach of US xenophobic nationalism. Undocumented people, for instance, are barred from earning time-earned credits, because their crime of "illegality," is described in the law as more grave than other offenses.

In addition to sentencing reform, we should reject another reigning bipartisan consensus—accepted even by many moderate liberals—which is that public prisons should be dismantled because they are too expensive. This argument exists on a slippery slope: When questions of justice are reduced to dollars and cents, margins and losses, risk and risk aversion, there is no reason why prisons might not be cost effective again at some future date. Privatized for-profit prisons, which now hold 10 percent of the nation's incarcerated people, are actually growing at an alarming rate: between 2000 and 2016 the private prison population increased five times faster than the entire prison population.[11]

We must also loudly say that racism isn't just an ugly belief but a system to be addressed with direct action and public policies. National Public Radio host Terry Gross recently asked Derek Black, a former prominent white supremacist who has denounced his racist views, whether he had "any guilt" about "other people who had committed violent acts and who espoused views that you had helped spread."[12] Gross's question reveals a cultural presumption that must be uprooted. Racism has political, social, and economic functions and benefits that have made it appealing to certain people for centuries; it is not, as Gross describes, a sick, disturbed, and nasty thought to feel guilty about. Had Gross had the insight to ask Black to consider how his prior support for white supremacy was linked to—and just the tip of the iceberg of—a long history of institutional racism in US society, then she would have helped her audience understand that racism isn't primarily a personal problem to be grappled with in the mind. The solution to systemic injustice isn't being more respectful with one another or being remorseful about past racist behavior. Transformation can only happen after we recognize what is true, ugly as it may be.

Another view we must work to overturn is expressed by ex-skinhead Christian Picciolini, who, of his work rehabilitating former neo-Nazis, says, "I had never in my life engaged in a meaningful dialogue with the people that I thought I hated, and it was these folks who showed me empathy when I least deserved it."[13] Like Black, Picciolini is courageous for speaking up about the false comforts of white supremacy. But, as history reveals, expressing empathy for racists is much less important than anti-racist action in the public sphere. The task isn't for Jews, blacks, Latinos, Muslims, and other members of groups targeted by bigots to be less judgmental and more tolerant toward those who wish to exterminate them. What is necessary is for the general public to forcefully call out neo-Nazi ideology as unacceptable. Ultimately, the solution doesn't rest upon the better moral behavior—the increased civility—of marginalized populations. The responsibility rests with white people who, knowingly or unknowingly, reap the benefits from their social power. They must be reformed and in turn demand a new vocabulary of political and social engagement.

Relatedly, few arguments are more in need of dismantling than the idea of reverse racism. According to white American public opinion, we don't live in a color-blind society. We live in a society in which black racists and their allies are discriminating against innocent whites. An NPR-Harvard University public opinion poll in October 2017 found that

55 percent of American whites think they are subject to racial discrimination, even though there is statistically no demonstrated antiwhite bias in any major economic, social, or cultural sector of the country.[14] There is a thin line between this view and what the right-wing fringe during the Obama presidency demanded as "white rights." The largely unchallenged rhetoric of reverse racism empowered the former Grand Wizard of the Louisiana Ku Klux Klan, David Duke—who ran unsuccessfully for the US Senate in 1990 and for governor of Louisiana in 1991—to complain bitterly in 2014, "If you simply defend the heritage of European-American people, then you're automatically a racist. There's massive racial discrimination against European-Americans."[15]

Civility grants racists inclusion in public discussion. But rejecting civil dialogue with reactionaries is the only way to prevent their views from being normalized. Take the example of American Enterprise Institute writer Charles Murray, whose notorious book *The Bell Curve* (1994), which he coauthored with Richard Herrnstein, used IQ test data to assert that black people are inherently less intelligent than white people. In 2014, on the twentieth anniversary of the book's publication, Murray restated his views, saying, "There is a mean difference in black and white scores on mental tests, historically about one standard deviation in magnitude on IQ tests . . . This difference is not the result of test bias, but reflects differences in cognitive functioning."[16]

When Murray expresses his beliefs in the public sphere, he can hide behind social science, methodology, and what he calls "empirical reality."[17] We know, however, that differences in IQ scores only prove the lack of adequate funding for black schools, unequal wealth distribution, and the culturally specific composition of standardized tests by test companies that measure traits that are valued in our economy.[18] They tell us nothing about people's natural intelligence. But those with a vested interest in maintaining the structures of inequality and injustice invoke the rules of civility to give Murray the benefit of the doubt, so he ignores any contravening evidence and goes on the offensive. He positions himself as a truth-teller, a number-crunching realist fighting "political correctness." And he claims to have benevolent intentions: He has stated that he wishes for black children with what he sees as genetically different skill sets to thrive by cutting government programs that he think are inefficient: "The point is not just to pass out enough money so that everyone has the means to live a decent existence. Rather, we need to live in a civil society that naturally creates valued places for people with many different kinds and levels of ability. In my experience, communities that are left alone to solve their own problems tend to produce those valued places."[19] This kind of reasoning echoes separate but equal Jim Crow segregationist assertions and is nothing but an update of pick-yourself-up-by-the-bootstraps individualism. Neither does anything to address racial domination. Instead, it only exacerbates racial inequality, while transferring responsibility for racial disparities from the white majority to the black minority.

Calling out racism in the public sphere is a must—and many social scientists have refuted Murray and Herrnstein's claims in the twenty years since *The Bell Curve* appeared. But memory, too, is powerful terrain for political action. In recent years, civic radicals have begun to develop greater public consciousness about the past as an antidote to romantic narratives about historical progress. The Mississippi Truth Project, organized through grassroots local chapters in 2009 to bring to the fore the racist violence in Mississippi during Jim Crow, is an outstanding example of such work. The goal of the activists involved in the project has been to collect oral histories about racist atrocities committed from 1945 to 1975, in an effort to get the state of Mississippi to create a truth commission.[20] Another is the Greensboro Truth and Reconciliation Commission (GTRC), organized in 2004, which shone a public spotlight on the Greensboro Massacre of November 3, 1979. On that day, members of the Ku Klux Klan and the American Nazi Party murdered five anti-Klan counterprotesters. Over the course of several years, the seven commissioners chosen by community organizers were tasked with hearing public and private testimony from participating former Klansmen and victims' families. The commission then compiled research that laid bare the truth of what had happened and crafted a description of the social conditions that had enabled white supremacist groups to form and act. In its final report, issued in 2006, the GTRC connected the past to the present, openly discussing the legacy of Jim Crow that still exists in the state, in police brutality against black citizens, unaffordable housing, and persistent racial segregation in both Greensboro and North Carolina at large.[21]

Whatever form future anti-racist projects take, they must be based in democratic ideas of social equality, unconditional freedom, and liberation for all. Such democratic ideas mobilize, organize, provoke, unsettle, and inspire citizens to express what they believe society will and will not stand for, what it will and will not aspire to, what is and is not tolerable. And when we say democracy, we mean a system in which people are able to rule themselves, individually and collectively with one another. For this reason, democracy isn't a narrow procedure that simply guarantees the right to vote—though, as we have seen, that right is itself under assault—or that supports a free and fair media.

Democracy isn't a dangerous form of populism in which mob rule wins the day. The Jim Crow South was no democracy, because black people couldn't participate freely in society. Trump's election wasn't an example of working-class populism gone awry, because millions of people couldn't even cast a vote against him. In some states, ex-felons were barred from voting, polling places were shut down, and severe voter ID laws turned voting into an endurance exercise of the will. Even more, some white workers in rural or post-industrial areas—whom the centrist class sees as responsible for Trump's election—were themselves swayed by Trump's liberal message of saving Social Security and Medicare because of what they lost after decades of antidemocratic privatization, austerity, and deregulation measures posing as utopia. So when we say democracy, we mean something that cuts against unbridled economic inequality, white supremacy, gender domination, transphobia, homophobia, and anti-immigrant nativism.

Central to achieving this democratic ideal is acting locally while thinking globally. This doesn't mean buying organic produce at the local farmers' market or fair trade coffee. It's something broader. Consider the recent Dakota Access Pipeline protests of 2016, which saw activists come to the sacred land of the Lakota Indians at Standing Rock, North Dakota, to resist the construction of an energy pipeline. Environmental degradation, these activists understood, disproportionately affects people of color, putting them at heightened risk for a host of health problems. But they also realized that what happens to the Lakota will soon be happening to the rest of us. Standing Rock for the government was a laboratory for conducting larger-scale destruction in the future.

Or think of the activists in Flint, Michigan, who described as environmental racism the process by which the city was put under emergency management in 2014 by Republican governor Rick Snyder, an act that led to the city's decision to switch its water source from the Detroit River to the Flint River. The subsequent mismanagement of this change allowed lead from the pipes into the drinking water, which poisoned thousands of children.

Activists at Standing Rock and in Flint knew that when it comes to building lasting coalitions and majorities, thinking intersectionally is key. Racial, gender, and economic oppression are interconnected because they come from the same root. Black and brown people, women, queer people, and poor people cannot struggle against systemic discrimination alone. They and their white allies make up the 99 percent. Ending mass incarceration adds newly enfranchised citizens to the population who can fight with workers for a living wage. Mobilizing against anti-LGBTQ sentiment creates a society in which no one will have to police their sexualities and identities to conform to some imagined norm.

Demilitarizing schools, defunding police departments, and ending the death penalty is the only way to transform a system that profits from death, social control, and punishment into one that respects citizens' inherent dignity. Political rights mean nothing without accessible healthcare for all, a living wage for workers, pensions for retirees, no-cost public college, affordable public housing, and myriad social programs such as food assistance, disability benefits, and retirement aid. Freedom from want creates a baseline for everyone to make reasoned and thoughtful choices about their lives. And without the concentration of labor power through public and private sector unions, this freedom will be endlessly under attack. Without this freedom, the people have little political power with which to influence policy.

All these aspirations are central to successful anti-racist movements because they go hand in hand with combating white supremacy. The whole class-versus-race opposition isn't a pressing problem but rather a red herring with little analytic value. Most left-leaning Americans know that antiblack racism does not affect everyone the same way; it uniquely destroys people of color. This incontestable fact—which, incidentally, anti-identity politics advocates vigorously deny—is consistent with the idea that economic equality is racial equality and racial equality is economic equality. The distinction between class and race creates a fake problem that forces activists into making unnecessary decisions and identifying with one at the expense of the other.

When it comes to protest tactics for civic radicals, history shows the power of direct nonviolent action—of strikes, protests, sit-ins, and boy-cotts—to transform the world. A politics based in armed self-defense, in contrast, is a boon to the profit-making interests of gun manufacturers and right-wing politicians. And more to the point, self-defense is a dangerous position in a society in which blackness is criminalized by police departments and in which vigilante citizens and stand your ground laws in many states effectively permit white people to shoot at will when they feel scared.

For decades, political centrism has peddled the dream of economic abundance without any cost, of post-racialism—the result of equal opportunities for all—being just around the corner, of the end of bitter ideological conflict. But inequality and exclusion have always been evident in American culture, and these conditions have always been maintained through violence. The plea for activists to be civil—in the past, now, and always—subverts this reality and implies that things can't really be that bad. After all, how can one even call for civility if catastrophe is staring one in the face? Isn't the call to civility a product of a smug insistence that individual moral virtue will magically fix an ailing society? It can't and it hasn't.

Civic radicals throughout US history have always known this fact to be true. As we prepare for politics beyond Trump, we must know that the battle for the future is won in the present—using lessons from the past, the connections among us, and our dreams of transformation.

In February 2017, leaders at Yale University decided to rename one of their fourteen residential colleges, Calhoun College, named in 1932 after one of its best-known graduates, John C. Calhoun, the nineteenth-century proslavery intellectual, US senator from South Carolina, and US vice president, who made his name denouncing abolitionist incivility and upholding slaveholder civility. The change at Yale came after months of weekly protest—held every Friday beginning in October 2016—planned by students and community activists as part of the Change the Name Coalition. At first, the university's administration was reticent, claiming the importance of hearing both sides of the issue and not cherry-picking negative historical facts about Calhoun but accepting the full range of traits, positive and negative, that exist in each person. Yale's president at the time, Peter Salovey, said, "Ours is a nation that often refuses to face its own history of slavery and racism. Yale is part of that history . . . We cannot erase American history but we can confront it, teach it, and learn from it. The decision to retain Calhoun College's name reflects the importance of this vital educational imperative."[22]

But this argument didn't persuade the many student protesters who showed up to the corner of Elm Street and New Haven Green each Friday, missed class, and got arrested and charged with misdemeanor disorderly conduct for barring traffic. Eventually the pressure was too great, and Yale's administration reversed course. When Yale changed the name of Calhoun College to Hopper College, in honor of the pioneering mathematician and computer scientist Grace Murray Hopper, the students won a small victory and received a minor concession, but a statue of Calhoun remained on campus, and alumni could continue to describe themselves as graduates of Calhoun College.

These protests were not an isolated act. In April 2017, eight graduate students at Yale went on a month-long hunger strike in front of President Salovey's home as representatives of their newly formed union, Local 33. Their goal was to begin the collective bargaining process with Yale—to which the institution was militantly opposed—in an effort to secure better pay, job security, greater respect as teachers, and access to child-care and healthcare. The graduate students also wanted stronger sexual harassment policies, given that a 2015 survey showed that 54 percent of female graduate students had experienced unwanted sexual advances at some point in their work.[23]

These students, like the undergraduates who fought to rename Calhoun College, faced an uphill battle in the face of daunting odds, as power never wants to give an inch. The power and resources on the two sides of the struggle were radically unequal. Yale's endowment stands at $25 billion, and its army of lawyers, mega-donors, and famous alumni will stop at nothing to secure its status as a factory of elite rule. But the Yale students had moral authority, numbers, passion, and vision. They weren't only thinking about short-term gains but a movement that constituted one step into a just future. Their aim was to create an ideal world on a small scale in New Haven that can be broadened until it is accessible to all. What they knew was that this was the truest form of civic radicalism. Civility wasn't an option for them, and it shouldn't be for the rest of us.

EPILOGUE

On May 25, 2020, a forty-six-year-old black man, George Floyd, was murdered in Minneapolis, Minnesota, by a white police officer, Derek Chauvin, who knelt on his neck for nearly nine minutes. Floyd was begging for mercy, calling for his deceased mother, and saying over and over again, "I can't breathe!" The event, which was captured on video by a bystander, had eerie echoes of the murder of another black man, Eric Garner, in Staten Island, New York, in 2014 when he, uttering the same words, "I can't breathe!" was strangled by a white police officer, Daniel Pantaleo. Garner's murder was met with outrage from Black Lives Matter activists, led to marches in major US cities, and received coverage in major US newspapers. But six years later, Floyd's killing sparked a noticeable change in American politics, leading to a mass movement against racism the likes of which we haven't seen since the 1960s. Demonstrations erupted in hundreds of cities—big and small—in the US and soon expanded globally, reaching the streets of Berlin, London, Seoul, and Melbourne. These marches would continue for weeks on end. They occurred at a moment when the novel coronavirus and its potentially fatal disease, COVID-19, had turned into a global pandemic, claiming hundreds of thousands of lives, shutting down large swaths of the world economy, and disproportionately affecting people of color. Remarkably, people showed up to protest Floyd's death and police brutality in general, even though many were under strict requirements and guidance from local governments and health officials to keep their distance from one another.

The immediate spark for the rebellion was Floyd's murder, which was the latest in a series of high-profile killings of innocent black men and women that caused national outrage. In March 2020, a black twenty-six-year-old emergency medical technician, Breonna Taylor, was shot by officers in Louisville, Kentucky, as they entered her apartment with a no-knock warrant. In February 2020, Ahmaud Arbery, a twenty-five-year-old black jogger, was out for his daily run and was shot by two white men, who had deputized themselves as neighborhood watchmen, becoming the judges, jury, and executioners.

Given protesters' pent-up rage after learning of these events—and years of watching similar incidents over and over again—it wasn't surprising that some of the early protests witnessed sporadic moments of violence, such as looting, arson, and destroyed property. And yet, some of the media coverage was narrowly focused on the protesters' violence, recalling again the civil versus uncivil distinctions elites have always used to interpret popular anti-racist uprisings throughout history. A CNN headline read "Protesters Break Curfew on Another Night of Fury and Frustrations over George Floyd's Killing," and a *Washington Post* article declared "A Night of Destruction Across D.C. After Protesters Clash with Police Outside White House."[1] In reading the coverage, one could see that history is everywhere. Recall how antislavery activists were told to be morally virtuous, how the black urban uprisings in Harlem, Watts, Detroit, and Newark in the 1960s were condemned, and how Martin Luther King's strategy of peaceful protest was elevated at every turn.

If there's one truth of US racial history, it's that the past is never truly past. But it would be a mistake to only look backward. What's happening today is a struggle over the future of American politics. Consider how much has changed over the past six years. During the Ferguson protests against the murder of Michael Brown in 2014 and the Baltimore uprisings in response to the killing in police custody of Freddie Gray in 2015, the mostly black protesters who chanted, "No Justice, No Peace!" were called terrorists and scolded for not listening to Barack Obama's calls for civility. And their phrase "Black Lives Matter" was met with the rebuke "Blue Lives Matter" or "All Lives Matter."

Not so today. We're seeing a multiracial movement led by youth that's critical not only of racism but of capitalism and patriarchy. Young black, brown, and white citizens—the future of the country—are now fearlessly on the streets asserting their voice. White citizens in particular have awoken from their moral slumber and are now acknowledging and disavowing the safety of white privilege. "Black Lives Matter" is hardly controversial now, having become a shorthand for declaring support for racial equality.

But rebellion never happens in a historical vacuum, without guidance from the past. Many of these multiracial youth have likely internalized Frederick Douglass's scathing critique of fake American patriotism amidst racial domination and James Baldwin's condemnation of white innocence in *The Fire Next Time*. Others have taken as nonnegotiable the intersectional thinking that Ida Wells and Audre Lorde believed was so vital. Growing up amidst the rise of mass incarceration since the 1980s, many Americans don't think it's all that radical to do what Angela Davis has been urging for years: abolish prisons. Having come of age in the wake of the 2008 Great Recession, young people don't see socialism as a boogeyman the way their grandparents might have. Like W. E. B. Du Bois, they believe a democratic society is consistent with a socialist economy in which working people control key decisions in the workplace, are guaranteed basic socioeconomic resources, and can live a meaningful life not driven by debilitating want.

When it comes to the old reactionary way of thinking, these young people have a kind of historical amnesia. And that's a good thing. Rather than shirk their responsibility to make democracy real, they stormed airports in 2017 in defiance of Trump's Muslim ban just months after he was inaugurated. And they have been on the front line of #MeToo and #NeverAgain, while raising the alarm about the ongoing climate change crisis and widening economic inequality.

Consider that in the aftermath of Garner's murder in 2014, talk of structural racism and racial domination was still seen as controversial and taboo, despite the fact that unarmed black men and women have been getting shot by police for centuries, that police departments have been heavily militarized since 9/11, and that broken-windows policing and stop and frisk have, for years, been reigning policies in many big cities. But today, thanks to collective pressure from below, we're seeing police unions condemning Floyd's murder; mayors and governors in red and blue states sympathizing with protesters; and major corporations like Target, CVS, and Nike refusing to condemn looting of their stores and instead pledging to help fight systemic racism. Even the media has begun highlighting the rogue and riotous behavior of cops and soldiers rather than exclusively bringing attention to disorderly protesters.

There's not only an unmistakable change in who is showing up for racial justice; noticeably different, too, is what the leaders of this anti-racist movement are demanding: pay reparations; divest from prisons and fossil fuels; and invest in the education, health, and safety of black people. It would have seemed unthinkable several years ago, but we're now hearing serious talk of defunding the police, which means either disbanding local police departments or shifting money from vast policing budgets toward mental health counseling and affordable housing. As of this writing, the Minneapolis city council has pledged to disband the city's police department. Many more communities are likely to take similar steps.

It's impossible to know what political victories and setbacks will come in the wake of these protests. After all, civic radical movements always face an uphill battle against the might of the state. But what we do know is the reason that today's activists have already won some early struggles is because they've taken to the streets and been disruptive. They have defied curfews, withstood police brutality at the barricades, blocked traffic, occupied city squares, and painted "Black Lives Matter" on city boulevards. Politicians and corporations haven't just coincidentally recognized the ills of their complicity in perpetuating racial inequality. They have been pushed to action, seeing the strength of the resistance that is growing unchecked from the grassroots.

For civic radicals, no longer is it tenable for law-and-order politics and moral apathy toward racial inequality—which have gripped the US since its founding—to continue unchecked. We're seeing the future of the nation play out before our eyes as these vocal citizens, marching with an immovable sense of moral purpose and staunch conviction in human liberation, write another chapter in US history and strive to make their freedom dreams our reality.

ACKNOWLEDGMENTS

All books require a great deal of support to be imagined and then, ultimately, completed. This one would have been impossible without a community of friends and colleagues who helped breathe life into this manuscript. I'm incredibly grateful to my agent, Matthew Carnicelli, whose boundless enthusiasm kept the project going at the beginning and whose keen and generous editorial eye helped shape its scope and narrative up until the end. My amazing editor at Beacon Press, Rachael Marks, exhibited a humbling level of dedication and commitment to the book. Her unmatched skill with the written word—in shaping sentences and tone and guiding the pacing of ideas—made the book what it is. To my colleagues and students at University of Detroit Mercy and my friends in academia and beyond, thank you for your ongoing support through the years. To my partner, the writer Alison Powell, thank you for urging me to do what I fear is impossible or foolhardy, and for showing me what it means to be brave. You were the original champion for this project, and none of it would have been possible without you. Finally, my children, Sam and Anita, have helped me grow as a person and have inspired me to always do better. It's to Alison, Sam, and Anita that I dedicate this work.

NOTES

CHAPTER 1: CIVILITY HAS NEVER BEEN NEUTRAL IN ITS USES AND IMPACTS

1. Alex Thomas, "Columnist Brooks Speaks at UC About Improving Political Civility," *West Virginia Metro News*, April 10, 2018, http://wvmetronews.com/2018/04/10/columnist-brooks-speaks-at-uc-about-improving-political-civility.

2. Clara Jeffery, "Van Jones: 'Hope for the Best, Expect and Prepare for the Worst,'" *Mother Jones*, November 14, 2016, https://www.motherjones.com/politics/2016/11/van-jones-donald-trump-sanders-clinton-racism.

3. Jessica Taylor, "Americans Say Civility Has Worsened Under Trump; Trust in Institutions Down" National Public Radio, July 03, 2017, https://www.npr.org/2017/07/03/535044005/americans-say-civility-has-worsened-under-trump-trust-in-institutions-down.

4. Michael S. Roth, "Political Correctness: Are the Kids on Campus Alright?" *Yale University Press Blog*, October 02, 2019, http://blog.yalebooks.com/2019/10/02/political-correctness-are-the-kids-on-campus-alright.

5. James Baldwin, "In Search of a Majority," *The Price of the Ticket: Collected Nonfiction, 1948–1985* (New York: St. Martin's Press, 1985), 235.

CHAPTER 2: CIVILITY DISTRACTS FROM INEQUALITY

1. John C. Calhoun, "Slavery a Positive Good," in *Abolition and Antislavery: A Historical Encyclopedia of the American Mosaic*, eds. Peter Hinks and John McKivigan (Santa Barbara: Greenwood, 2015), 395. Calhoun held out the threat of Southern seccession when he became the first person to resign the vice presidency, in 1832, to support his home state of South Carolina when it wanted to unilaterally render null and void federal tariffs in what became known as the Nullification Crisis. But anyone could see the writing on the wall. On March 22, 1833, the US Congress passed the Force Bill that gave the Democratic president, Jackson, authority to use military intervention to make South Carolina comply with the federal government. This was but the latest step in strengthening the federal government after the *McCulloch v. Maryland* (1819) Supreme Court decision. Federalist Chief Justice John Marshall—though a slaveholder himself—penned the ruling in favor of the federal government over the state of Maryland regarding the incorporation of a federal bank. Things were not boding well for slaveholders. States' rights arguments were on thinner ground than ever before.

2. George C. Fitzhugh, *Cannibals All! Or, Slaves Without Masters* (Bedford, MA: Applewood Books, 1857), 55.

3. Fitzhugh, *Cannibals All!*, 284.

4. Herbert Aptheker, *American Negro Slave Revolts* (New York: International Publishers, 1983), 72, 62.

5. Aptheker, *American Negro Slave Revolts*, 327.

6. Jon Meacham, *Thomas Jefferson: The Art of Power* (New York: Random House, 2012), 326.

7. Thomas Jefferson, *Notes on the State of Virginia* (New York: Penguin, 1999), 146.

8. William Gilmore Simms, *Proslavery Argument* (Philadelphia: Lippincott, Grambo and Co., 1852), 206.

9. William Harper, *Memoir on Slavery* (Charleston: James Burges, 1838), 20.

10. Thomas Jefferson, *The Jefferson Papers*, vol. 7 (Princeton, NJ: Princeton University Press, 1953), 356.

11. Frederick Douglass, "'I Love You but Hate Slavery': Frederick Douglass to His Former Owner, Hugh Auld, 1857," Gilder Lehrman Institute of American History, October 4, 1857, http://ap.gilderlehrman.org/resources/%C3%A2%E2%82%AC%C5%93i-love-you-hate-slavery%C3%A2%E2%82%AC%C2%9D-frederick-douglass-his-f?period=5.

12. Frederick Douglass, "What to the Slave Is the Fourth of July?," in *The Essential Douglass: Selected Writings and Speeches*, ed. Nicholas Buccola (Indianapolis: Hackett Press, 2016), 67.

13. David Blight, *Frederick Douglass: Prophet of Freedom* (New York: Simon & Schuster, 2018), 240.

14. Blight, *Frederick Douglass*, 239.

15. William Lloyd Garrison, *Thoughts on African Colonization* (Boston: Garrison and Knapf, 1832), 21.

16. Julie Winch, *A Gentleman of Color: The Life of James Forten* (New York: Oxford University Press, 2003), 71.

17. Donald Yacovone, *Samuel Joseph May and the Dilemmas of the Liberal Persuasion, 1797–1871* (Philadelphia: Temple University Press, 1991), 135; quoted in Len Gougeon, "Militant Abolitionism: Douglass, Emerson, and the Rise of the Anti-Slave," *New England Quarterly* 85, no. 4 (December 2012): 648.

18. Frederick Douglass, *My Bondage and My Freedom*, in *Douglass: Autobiographies*, ed. Henry Louis Gates Jr. (New York: Library of America, 1994), 286.

19. William Lloyd Garrison, *No Compromise with Slavery* (New York: American Anti-Slavery Society, 1854), 14.

20. Henry Mayer, *All on Fire: William Lloyd Garrison and the Abolition of Slavery* (New York: St. Martin's Press, 1988), 121; quoted in Tony Horowitz, *Midnight Rising: John Brown and the Raid That Sparked the Civil War* (New York: Henry Holt, 2011), 24.

21. Blight, *Frederick Douglass*, 247.

22. Harriet Beecher Stowe, *Uncle Tom's Cabin: Or, Life Among the Lowly* (New York: Houghton, Mifflin and Company, 1891), 303. Even when, in 1856, Stowe wrote her second novel, *Dred: A Tale of the Great Dismal Swamp*—partly based on mystical preacher and rebel Nat Turner—she couldn't resist making the protagonist, Dred, a Christian healer. Dred's work is done not through direct action against the slaveholder

whips but by helping fugitive slaves elude capture. The revolutionary promise that framed the novel was nowhere in sight, and Dred sounded less like Turner and more like Uncle Tom when he said, "And the King shall reign in righteousness. He shall redeem their souls from deceit and violence. He shall sit upon a white cloud, and the rainbow shall be round about his head." Harriet Beecher Stowe, *Dred: A Tale of the Great Dismal Swamp* (New York: Sully and Kleinteich, 1884), 539.

23. Walt Whitman, *Poetry and Prose* (New York: Library of America, 1982), 1174.

24. Whitman, *Poetry and Prose*, 35–36.

25. David S. Reynolds, *John Brown, Abolitionist: The Man Who Killed Slavery, Sparked the Civil War, and Seeded Civil Rights* (New York: Vintage, 2005), 53–54.

26. Henry Clay, *The Works of Henry Clay* (New York: G. P. Putnam and Sons, 1904), 464–65.

27. See Alex Zamalin, *Struggle on Their Minds: The Political Thought of African American Resistance* (New York: Columbia University Press, 2017), 25–48.

28. David Walker, *Walker's Appeal, in Four Articles; Together with a Preamble, to the Coloured Citizens of the World, but in Particular, and Very Expressly, to Those of the United States of America*, Documenting the American South, University Library of the University of North Carolina–Chapel Hill, http://docsouth.unc.edu/nc/walker/menu.html.

29. Reynolds, *John Brown, Abolitionist*, 152.

30. As Reynolds writes, "Thousands of Missourians were ready at election time to go into Kansas, take over the polling booths there, and cast their ballots for proslavery candidates." *John Brown, Abolitionist*, 141.

31. Blight, *Frederick Douglass*, 302.

32. Blight, *Frederick Douglass*, 309.

33. Henry David Thoreau, "A Plea for Captain John Brown," in *The Writings of Henry David Thoreau*, vol. 4 (New York: Houghton Mifflin, 1906), 413.

34. Henry David Thoreau, "Resistance to Civil Government," in *Political Writings*, ed. Nancy Rosenblum (Cambridge, MA: Cambridge University Press, 1996), 7.

35. Beverly Lowry, *Harriet Tubman: Imagining a Life* (New York: Anchor, 2008), 200.

36. Reynolds, *John Brown, Abolitionist*, 259.

37. Nell Irvin Painter, *Sojourner Truth: A Life, a Symbol* (New York: Norton, 1997), 98.

38. Maria W. Stewart, *Maria W. Stewart: America's First Black Woman Political Writer: Essays and Speeches*, ed. Marilyn Richardson (Bloomington: Indiana University Press, 1987), 46–47.

39. Frederick Douglass, "The President and His Speeches," *Douglass' Monthly*, September 1862, in *Frederick Douglass: Selected Speeches and Writings*, ed. Philip Foner and Yuval Taylor (Chicago: Chicago Review Press, 2000), 513.

40. Abraham Lincoln, *Speeches and Writings, 1832–1858*, ed. Don E. Fehrenbacher (New York: Library of America, 1974), 33.

41. Abraham Lincoln, *Abraham Lincoln's Speeches* (New York: Dodd, Mead and Company, 1895), 211.

42. Blight, *Frederick Douglass*, 474.

43. Andrew Johnson, *The Papers of Andrew Johnson*, vol. 10, *February–July 1866* (Knoxville: University of Tennessee Press, 1992), 48.

44. David Blight, *Race and Reunion: The Civil War in American Memory* (Cambridge, MA: Harvard University Press, 2002), 99.

45. Blight, *Race and Reunion*, 215.

46. Blight, *Frederick Douglass*, 491. Stanton became angered, and, despicably, turned to racism as a political strategy in an attempt to elevate women's suffrage in public opinion. She played upon white anxiety by asking what would it mean if "Sambo," who hadn't read the Declaration of Independence, could vote; later, in February 1869, she stoked fear by equating black enfranchisement with sexual violence, arguing that it would "culminate in fearful outrages on womanhood." This reprehensible line of reasoning was indefensible. Never is strategic racism acceptable to get a point across, no matter how progressive the cause. Racist strategies can only leave behind a residue of the vicious, hierarchical thinking that will—over time—infect and undermine a society striving toward equality for all. But Stanton could have easily made her political criticism without using racism: why not build a sustainable broad-based mass movement for black men and all women rather than secure a single victory for women's voting rights?

CHAPTER 3: CIVIC RADICALS MAKE DO WITH WHAT THEY HAVE

1. Booker T. Washington, "The Standard Printed Version of the Atlanta Exposition Address," in *The Booker T. Washington Papers*, ed. Louis R. Harlan (Urbana: University of Illinois Press, 1972), 584.

2. Booker T. Washington, "Christmas Days in Old Virginia," *Suburban Life* (July 1907): 336–38.

3. Joel Chandler Harris, *The Complete Tales of Uncle Remus* (New York: Houghton Mifflin, 2002), xxvii. In Chandler's view, *Uncle Tom's Cabin* was a flawed but redeeming work that revealed Stowe's tortured desire to condemn slavery in Kentucky alongside something in it that "attacked her sympathy," so that no "unprejudiced person" can "fail to see in it a defense of slavery." See Julia Collier, *Joel Chandler Harris: Editor and Essayist* (Chapel Hill: University Press of North Carolina, 1931), 116.

4. Quoted in Leon Litwack, *Trouble in Mind: Black Southerners in the Age of Jim Crow* (New York: Vintage Books, 1999), 188.

5. Thomas Nelson Page, *The Negro: The Southerner's Problem* (New York: Charles Scribner's Sons, 1904), 166; 80.

6. Litwack, *Trouble in Mind*, 225.

7. William A. Dunning, "The Undoing of Reconstruction," *Atlantic Monthly*, October 1901, 437–38.

8. Alfred Waddell, "Colonel Alfred M. Waddell Justifies a Race Riot, 1898," in *Documenting American Violence: A Sourcebook*, ed. Christopher Waldrep and Michael Bellesiles (New York: Oxford University Press, 2005), 197.

9. Rob Christensen, *The Paradox of Tar Heel Politics: The Personalities, Elections, and Events that Shaped Modern North Carolina* (Chapel Hill: University of North Carolina Press, 2008), 26.

10. William McKinley, "First Inaugural Address," March 4, 1897, available at https://avalon.law.yale.edu/19th_century/mckin1.asp.

11. Emma Lou Thornbrough, *T. Thomas Fortune: Militant Journalist* (Chicago: University of Chicago Press, 1972), 182.

12. Thornbrough, *T. Thomas Fortune*, 106.

13. Thornbrough, *T. Thomas Fortune*, 108.

14. Thornbrough, *T. Thomas Fortune*, 46.

15. Thornbrough, *T. Thomas Fortune*, 48.

16. Thornbrough, *T. Thomas Fortune*, 81.

17. William Graham Sumner, *What Social Classes Owe Each Other* (Caldwell, ID: Caxton Printers, 1952), accessed via Mises Institute Library, https://cdn.mises.org/What%20Social%20Classes%20Owe%20Each%20Other_2.pdf, 22; 55.

18. Timothy Thomas Fortune, *Black and White: Land, Labor, and Politics in the South* (New York: Fords, Howard and Hulbert, 1884), 234. See Susan D. Carle, *Defining the Struggle: National Organizing for Racial Justice, 1880–1915* (New York: Oxford University Press, 2013), 41.

19. Fortune, *Black and White*, iv. See Carle, *Defining the Struggle*, 41.

20. Booker T. Washington, *Booker T. Washington Papers*, vol. 9, *1906–1908*, ed. Lewis Harlan and Raymond Smock (Urbana: University of Illinois Press, 1980), 76.

21. Booker T. Washington, *Booker T. Washington Papers*, vol. 8, *1904–1906*, ed. Lewis Harlan and Raymond Smock (Urbana: University of Illinois Press, 1979), 671.

22. Booker T. Washington, *Booker T. Washington Papers*, vol. 7, *1903–1904*, ed. Lewis Harlan and Raymond Smock (Urbana: University of Illinois Press, 1979), 447.

23. Booker T. Washington, *Booker T. Washington Papers*, vol. 9, *1906–1908*, 249.

24. Robert J. Norrell, *Up from History: The Life of Booker T. Washington* (Cambridge, MA: Harvard University Press, 2011), 113–14.

25. Anthony Slide, *American Racist: The Life and Films of Thomas Dixon* (Lexington: University Press of Kentucky, 2004), 64.

26. Thomas Dixon, *The Leopard's Spots* (New York: Grosset & Dunlap, 1902), 368.

27. Stephen Kantrowitz, *Ben Tillman and the Reconstruction of White Supremacy* (Chapel Hill: University of North Carolina Press, 2000).

28. Ben Tillman, "Lynch Law," *The Congressional Record—Senate*, 59th Cong., 2nd Sess., vol. 41, pt. 2 (January 1907): 1441.

29. Jane Addams, "Respect for Law," *Independent*, no. 2718, January 3, 1901, 18; 20.

30. William James, "A Strong Note of Warning Regarding the Lynching Epidemic" (1903), in *Essays, Comments and Reviews* (Cambridge, MA: Harvard University Press, 1987), 173; 172.

31. Ida B. Wells, *Southern Horrors: Lynch Law in All Its Phases* (1892), available at http://www.digitalhistory.uh.edu/disp_textbook.cfm?smtid=3&psid=3614.

32. Wells, *Southern Horrors*.

33. Mia Bay, *To Tell the Truth Freely: The Life of Ida B. Wells* (New York: Hill and Wang, 2010), 143–50.

34. Bay, *To Tell the Truth Freely*, 116.

35. See David Levering Lewis, *W. E. B. Du Bois: Biography of a Race, 1868–1919* (New York: Henry Holt, 1993), 336.

36. W. E. B. Du Bois, *The Souls of Black Folk* (1903' repr. New York: Dover, 1994), 7.

37. Kerri K. Greenidge, *Black Radical: The Life and Times of William Monroe Trotter* (New York: Liveright, 2019), 118.

38. David F. Krugler, *1919, The Year of Racial Violence: How African Americans Fought Back* (New York: Cambridge University Press, 2014), 260.

39. Alfred L. Brophy, *Reconstructing the Dreamland: The Tulsa Riot of 1921* (New York: Oxford University Press, 2003), 46.

40. William M. Tuttle Jr., *Race Riot: Chicago in the Red Summer of 1919* (Urbana: University of Illinois Press, 1970), 172.

41. Quoted in Claire Hartfield, *A Few Red Drops: The Chicago Race Riot of 1919* (New York: Clarion, 2018), 137.

42. See *St. Louis Post-Dispatch*, July 7, 1917.

43. W. E. B. Du Bois, *Darkwater: Voices from Within the Veil* (1920) (New York: Dover, 2012), 59.

44. Joseph Gerteis, *Class and the Color Line: Interracial Class Coalition in the Knights of Labor and the Populist Movement* (Durham, NC: Duke University Press, 2007), 45.

45. Daniel Rosenberg, *New Orleans Dockworkers: Race, Labor, and Unionism* (Albany: State University of New York, 1988), 34–35.

46. Frances Fox Piven and Richard Cloward, *Poor People's Movements: Why They Succeed, How They Fail* (New York: Vintage, 1979), 54–55.

47. Piven and Cloward, *Poor People's Movements*, 56–57.

48. Nell Irvin Painter, *The Narrative of Hosea Hudson: The Life and Times of a Black Radical* (New York: Norton, 1979), 101.

49. Ida B. Wells, *Crusade for Justice: The Autobiography of Ida B. Wells* (Chicago: University of Chicago Press, 1970), 415.

CHAPTER 4: CIVIC RADICALS SPEAK TRUTH TO POWER

1. James Baldwin, "Smaller than Life," in *Collected Essays* (New York: Library of America, 1998), 577–78.

2. James Baldwin, "James Baldwin Discusses His Book *Nobody Knows My Name: More Notes from a Native Son*" (interview), July 15, 1961, Studs Terkel Radio Archive, Chicago History Museum, digital audio from reel-to-reel tape, 51:13, https://studsterkel.wfmt.com/programs/james-baldwin-discusses-his-book-nobody-knows-my-name-more-notes-native-son.

3. Lillian Smith, *Killers of the Dream* (New York: Norton, 1949), 16.

4. Smith, *Killers of the Dream*, 222.

5. James Baldwin, "Many Thousands Gone," in *Collected Essays* (New York: Library of America, 1998), 22.

6. William Faulkner, *Essays, Speeches & Public Letters* (New York: Modern Library, 2004), 87.

7. Milton Friedman, *Capitalism and Freedom* (Chicago: University of Chicago Press, 2002).

8. Gary Becker, *The Economics of Discrimination* (orig. 1957; Chicago: University of Chicago Press, 1971).

9. Quoted in Berry Craig, "Right to Work Founder was a Klan Fan," AFL-CIO, August 22, 2017, https://aflcio.org/2017/8/22/right-work-founder-was-klan-fan.

10. Friedman, *Capitalism and Freedom*, 111.

11. Ayn Rand, "Racism," in *The Virtue of Selfishness* (New York: Signet, 1964), 152.

12. Norman Podhoretz, "My Negro Problem—and Ours," in *The Norman Podhoretz Reader*, ed. Thomas L. Jeffers (New York: Free Press, 2004), 61; 59.

13. James Baldwin, "Faulkner and Desegregation," in *Collected Essays* (New York: Library of America, 1998), 214.

14. James Baldwin, *The Fire Next Time*, in *Collected Essays* (New York: Library of America, 1998), 341.

15. James Baldwin, "The Dangerous Road Before Martin Luther King," in *Collected Essays* (New York: Library of America, 1998), 641.

16. Martin Luther King Jr., "I Have a Dream" (1963), in *A Testament of Hope*, ed. James M. Washington (San Francisco: Harper Collins, 1986), 218–19.

17. Martin Luther King Jr., "Letter from a Birmingham Jail" (1963), in *A Testament of Hope*, ed. James M. Washington (San Francisco: Harper Collins, 1986), 295.

18. "Statement by Alabama Clergymen," April 12, 1963, Estate of Martin Luther King, Jr., https://swap.stanford.edu/20141218230016/http://mlk-kpp01.stanford.edu/kingweb/popular_requests/frequentdocs/clergy.pdf.

19. John Herbers, "Dr. King Rebuts Hoover Charges," *New York Times*, November 20, 1964.

20. This episode is captured in Robert Weisbrot, *Freedom Bound: A History of America's Civil Rights Movement* (New York: Norton, 1989), 56–58.

21. Weisbrot, *Freedom Bound*, 39.

22. David Leeming, *James Baldwin: A Biography* (New York: Knopf, 1994), 222–25.

23. Leeming, *James Baldwin*, 224.

24. James Baldwin, "Everybody's Protest Novel," in *Collected Essays* (New York: Library of America, 1998), 11.

25. Quoted in Herb Boyd, *James Baldwin's Harlem: A Biography of James Baldwin* (New York: Atria Books, 2008), 77.

26. Robert Cohen, *Freedom's Orator: Mario Savio and the Radical Legacy of the 1960s* (New York: Oxford University Press, 2014), 100.

27. Gerald Horne, *Fire This Time: The Watts Uprising and the 1960s* (Charlottesville: University of Virginia Press, 1995).

28. Joel Stone, ed., *Detroit 1967: Origins, Impacts, Legacies* (Detroit: Wayne State University Press, 2017).

29. Daryl Michael Scott, *Contempt and Pity: Social Policy and the Image of the Damaged Black Psyche, 1880–1996* (Chapel Hill: University of North Carolina Press, 1997), 147.

30. Scott, *Contempt and Pity*, 147.

31. Quoted in Marisa Chappell, *The War on Welfare: Family, Poverty, and the Politics of Modern America* (Philadelphia: University of Pennsylvania Press, 2010), 49.

32. Gunnar Myrdal, *An American Dilemma: The Negro Problem and Modern Democracy* (New York: Harper, 1944), 949.

33. James Baldwin, "The American Dream and the American Negro," in *Collected Essays* (New York: Library of America, 1998), 718.

34. Baldwin, "The American Dream and the American Negro," 718; 719.

35. Matthew Frye Jacobson, *Roots Too: White Ethnic Revival in the Post–Civil Rights Era* (Cambridge, MA: Harvard University Press, 2008).

36. Podhoretz, "My Negro Problem—And Ours," 59.

37. Michael Novak, *Unmeltable Ethnics: Politics and Culture in American Life* (orig. 1972; New Brunswick, NJ: Transaction Publishers, 1996), xliv.

38. Ira Katznelson, *When Affirmative Action Was White: An Untold History of Racial Inequality in Twentieth-Century America* (New York: Norton, 2005), 114.

39. James Baldwin, "White Man's Guilt," in *Collected Essays* (New York: Library of America, 1998), 723.

40. Quoted in Weisbrot, *Freedom Bound*, 203.

41. Martin Luther King Jr., "Where Do We Go from Here?," speech, Eleventh Annual SCLC Convention, August 16, 1967, available at Martin Luther King Jr. Research and Education Institute, Stanford University, https://kinginstitute.stanford.edu/king-papers/documents/where-do-we-go-here-address-delivered-eleventh-annual-sclc-convention.

42. Quoted in Boyd, *James Baldwin's Harlem*, 77.

43. Willie Morris, *Conversations with Willie Morris*, ed. Jack Bales (Jackson: University Press of Mississippi, 2000), 114.

44. Willie Morris, *North Toward Home* (Boston: Houghton Mifflin, 1967), 403; 385–86.

45. Quoted in Fred Hobson, "The Southern Racial Conversion Narrative: Larry L. King and Pat Waters," *Virginia Quarterly Review* 75, no. 2 (Spring 1999), https://www.vqronline.org/essay/southern-racial-conversion-narrative-larry-l-king-and-pat-watters.

46. James Boggs, *The American Revolution: Pages from a Negro Worker's Notebook* (New York: Monthly Review Press, 1963), 90.

47. Malcolm X, "Racism: The Cancer That Is Destroying America," in *Malcolm X: The Man and His Times*, ed. John Henrik Clarke (Trenton, NJ: Africa World Press, 1990), 304.

48. Malcolm X, "Organization of Afro-American Unity: A Statement of Basic Aims and Objectives," in *Malcolm X: The Man and His Times*, ed. John Henrik Clarke (Trenton, NJ: Africa World Press, 1990), 340.

49. James Baldwin, *No Name on the Street*, in *Collected Essays* (New York: Library of America, 1998), 412.

50. Quoted in Weisbrot, *Freedom Bound*, 135.

CHAPTER 5: CIVIC RADICALS BELIEVE RACISM IS STRUCTURAL RATHER THAN PERSONAL

1. James Baldwin, "An Open Letter to My Sister, Miss Angela Davis," *New York Review of Books*, January 7, 1971, https://www.nybooks.com/articles/1971/01/07/an-open-letter-to-my-sister-miss-angela-davis.

2. Richard Nixon, "Address Accepting the Presidential Nomination at the Republican National Convention in Miami Beach, Florida," August 8, 1968, https://www.presidency.ucsb.edu/documents/address-accepting-the-presidential-nomination-the-republican-national-convention-miami?.

3. Carol Anderson, *White Rage: The Unspoken Truth of Our Racial Divide* (New York: Bloomsbury, 2016), chapter 4.

4. John Abt, "From New York to California: The Extradition of Angela Y. Davis," in *If They Come in the Morning: Voices of Resistance*, ed. Angela Y. Davis (New York: Verso, 2016), chapter 21.

5. Bettina Aptheker, *The Morning Breaks: The Trial of Angela Davis* (Ithaca, NY: Cornell University Press, 2014), xi.

6. "The Angela Davis Tragedy," *New York Times*, October 16, 1970, https://www.nytimes.com/1970/10/16/archives/the-angela-davis-tragedy.html.

7. Sam Roberts, "Rockefeller on the Attica Raid, from Boastful to Subdued," *New York Times*, September 12, 2011, https://www.nytimes.com/2011/09/13/nyregion/rockefeller-initially-boasted-to-nixon-about-attica-raid.html.

8. American Civil Liberties Union, "Cracks in the System: 20 Years of the Unjust Federal Crack Cocaine Law," October 2006, https://www.aclu.org/other/cracks-system-20-years-unjust-federal-crack-cocaine-law?.

9. George L. Kelling and James Q. Wilson, "Broken Windows: The Police and Neighborhood Safety," *Atlantic Monthly*, March 1982, https://www.theatlantic.com/magazine/archive/1982/03/broken-windows/304465.

10. John DiIulio, "The Coming of the Super-Predators," *Weekly Standard*, November 27, 1995, https://www.weeklystandard.com/john-j-dilulio-jr/the-coming-of-the-super-predators.

11. See Lydia Saad, "Military, Small Business, Police Still Stir Most Confidence," Gallup, https://news.gallup.com/poll/236243/military-small-business-police-stir-confidence.aspx.

12. National Advisory Commission on Civil Disorders, *The Kerner Report*, 1968 (Princeton, NJ: Princeton University Press, 2016), 2.

13. Lawrence Mead, *Beyond Entitlement: The Social Obligations of Citizenship* (New York: Free Press, 1986), 43.

14. Sam Dolnick, "The Life and Crimes of America's Original Welfare Queen," *New York Times*, May 20, 2019, https://www.nytimes.com/2019/05/20/books/review/josh-levin-queen-linda-taylor.html.

15. Mead, *Beyond Entitlement*, 22.

16. Dinesh D'Souza, *The End of Racism: Principles for a Multiracial Society* (New York: Free Press, 1995), 484, 485.

17. Shelby Steele, *The Content of Our Character: A New Vision of Race in America* (New York: Harper, 1999), 52–53.

18. Steele, *The Content of Our Character*, 52.

19. John McWhorter, *Losing the Race: Self-Sabotage in Black America* (New York: Free Press, 2000), 61–62.

20. Ben Carson and Candy Carson, *One Nation: What We Can All Do to Save America's Future* (New York: Sentinel, 2014), 17.

21. Alexis De Veaux, *Warrior Poet: A Biography of Audre Lorde* (New York: Norton, 2006), 331.

22. Audre Lorde, *Sister Outsider: Essays and Speeches* (New York: Penguin, 2020), 129.

23. Lorde, *Sister Outsider*, 46.

24. De Veaux, *Warrior Poet*, 244.

25. This bill was fifty years in the making. As political scientist Naomi Murakawa compellingly demonstrates, Richard Nixon's law-and-order platform that got him elected in 1968, in which he implicitly defined black-on-white crime as a consequence of 1960s urban uprisings, has roots in the Democratic progressive policy platform introduced by president Harry Truman, whose groundbreaking Committee on Civil Rights in 1948 made as a central objective the "right to safety" in order to "control bias

in criminal justice administration." The problem was that laws like Truman's that were originally meant to protect black people from white violence were eventually transformed and used against black people instead, to "protect" white people from them. See Naomi Murakawa, *The First Civil Right: How Liberals Built Prison America* (New York: Oxford University Press, 2014), 3.

26. Martin Crutsinger, "Wage Stagnation Worsens in '90s, Study Shows," *Washington Post*, September 1, 1996, https://www.washingtonpost.com/archive/politics /1996/09/01/wage-stagnation-worsens-in-90s-study-shows/28163ed7-e9d7–48a8–9803 -eaf63d982053.

27. Jon Swaine and Ciara McCarthy, "Young Black Men Again Faced Highest Rate of US Police Killings in 2016," *Guardian*, June 8, 2017, https://www.theguardian.com /us-news/2017/jan/08/the-counted-police-killings-2016-young-black-men.

28. "Congress Apologizes for Slavery, Jim Crow," National Public Radio, July 30, 2008, https://www.npr.org/templates/story/story.php?storyId=93059465.

29. US Senate, "S. Res. 39 (109th): Lynching Victims Senate Apology Resolution," June 13, 2005, https://www.govtrack.us/congress/bills/109/sres39/text.

30. George W. Bush, "Remarks on Compassionate Conservatism in San Jose, California," in *Public Papers of the Presidents of the United States: George W. Bush* (Washington, DC: US Government Publishing Office, April 30, 2002), 694.

31. George W. Bush, "State of the Union Address," White House Archives, January 31, 2006, https://georgewbush-whitehouse.archives.gov/stateoftheunion/2006.

32. Charles P. Pierce, "A Catholic Nun Schooled Paul Ryan in Humility Last Night," *Esquire*, August 22, 2017, https://www.esquire.com/news-politics/politics /news/a57140/paul-ryan-nun-town-hall.

33. Angela Y. Davis, *Are Prisons Obsolete?* (New York: Seven Stories Press, 2003), 107–8.

34. Barack Obama, "Father's Day Remarks," June 15, 2008, *New York Times*, https://www.nytimes.com/2008/06/15/us/politics/15text-obama.html.

35. Barack Obama and Shinzo Abe, "Remarks by President Obama and Prime Minister Abe of Japan in Joint Press Conference," April 28, 2015, https://obamawhite-house.archives.gov/the-press-office/2015/04/28/remarks-president-obama-and-prime -minister-abe-japan-joint-press-confere.

36. Lisa Snowden-McCray, "A Look Back at the Reign of Stephanie Rawlings-Blake," *Baltimore Sun*, December 14, 2016, https://www.baltimoresun.com/citypaper /bcp-121416-mobs-srb-20161214-story.html.

37. Rod Dreher, "Zimmerman Trial Idiocy," *American Conservative*, June 28, 2013, https://www.theamericanconservative.com/dreher/zimmerman-trial-idiocy.

38. Rod Dreher, "Tips for Not Getting Shot by Cops," *American Conservative*, November 29, 2014, https://www.theamericanconservative.com/dreher/tips-for-not -getting-shot-by-cops.

39. Terrence McCoy, "Ferguson Shows How a Police Force Can Turn into a Plundering 'Collection Agency,'" *Washington Post*, March 05, 2015, https://www.washington post.com/news/morning-mix/wp/2015/03/05/ferguson-shows-how-a-police-force-can -turn-into-a-plundering-collection-agency.

40. Richard Luscombe, "George Zimmerman: A Wannabe Cop 'Sick and Tired' of Criminals, Court Hears," *Guardian*, July 12, 2013, https://www.theguardian.com /world/2013/jul/12/george-zimmerman-trayvon-martin-murder-trial.

41. Paul Solotaroff, "A Most American Way to Die," *Rolling Stone*, April 25, 2013, https://www.rollingstone.com/culture/culture-news/trayvon-martin-stand-your-ground-florida-jordan-davis-93561.

42. David Wilson, *Inventing Black-on-Black Violence: Discourse, Space, and Representation* (Syracuse, NY: Syracuse University Press, 2005).

43. Lisa L. Miller, "Black Activists Don't Ignore Crime," *New York Times*, August 5, 2016, https://www.nytimes.com/2016/08/06/opinion/black-activists-dont-ignore-crime.html.

44. Julian Hattem, "FBI Head Doubles Down on 'Ferguson Effect,'" *Hill*, November 13, 2015, https://thehill.com/policy/national-security/260080-fbi-head-doubles-down-on-ferguson-effect.

45. Heather Mac Donald, "Heather Mac Donald on Black Lives Matter: Does the Truth Matter?" *Real Clear Politics*, posted by Tim Hains, September 23, 2016, https://www.realclearpolitics.com/video/2016/09/23/heather_macdonald_on_black_lives_matter_does_the_truth_matter.html.

46. Julia Craven, "32 Blue Lives Matter Bills Have Been Introduced Across 14 States This Year," *Huffington Post*, December 11, 2017, https://www.huffpost.com/entry/blue-black-lives-matter-police-bills-states_n_58b61488e4b0780bac2e31b8.

47. Nicholas Kristof, "Race, the Police, and the Propaganda," *New York Times*, January 10, 2015, https://www.nytimes.com/2015/01/11/opinion/sunday/nicholas-kristof-race-the-police-and-the-propaganda.html.

48. Johnny Kaufmann, "Georgia Law Allows Tens of Thousands to Be Wiped from Voter Rolls," National Public Radio, October 22, 2018, https://www.npr.org/2018/10/22/659416485/georgia-s-use-it-or-lose-it-law-wipes-voters-from-rolls.

49. Jane Mayer, "The Voter-Fraud Myth," *New Yorker*, October 22, 2012, https://www.newyorker.com/magazine/2012/10/29/the-voter-fraud-myth.

50. Ilya Somin, "The Ignorant Voter," interview by Jared Meyer, *Forbes*, June 27, 2016, https://www.forbes.com/sites/jaredmeyer/2016/06/27/american-voters-are-ignorant-but-not-stupid/#58dcdac57ff1.

51. For an account of this movement see William J. Barber II and Jonathan Wilson-Hartgrove, *The Third Reconstruction: How a Moral Movement Is Overcoming the Politics of Division and Fear* (Boston: Beacon Press, 2016).

52. Barber and Wilson-Hartgrove, *The Third Reconstruction*, 126.

CHAPTER 6: CIVILITY IS DEPLOYED WHEN DEMOCRATIC MOVEMENTS ARE ON THE RISE AND REACTIONARIES ARE ON THE ROPES

1. Dahlia Lithwick, "The Decade Civility Died, and 'Civility' Replaced It," *Slate*, December 20, 2019, https://slate.com/news-and-politics/2019/12/decade-civility-died-2010s-donald-trump.html.

2. Jonathan Zimmerman, "Promoting Civility in Washington in the Age of Trump," WHYY, June 22, 2017, https://whyy.org/articles/essay-promoting-civility-in-washington-in-the-age-of-trump.

3. Isadora Rangel, "'Socialist,' 'Racist' . . . What Happens When Liberals and Conservatives Drop Stereotypes?" *USA Today*, April 10, 2019, https://www.usatoday.com/story/opinion/2019/04/10/civility-brevard-aims-help-liberals-conservatives-drop-stereotypes/3410466002.

4. "Center for Immigration Studies," Southern Poverty Law Center, https://www
.splcenter.org/fighting-hate/extremist-files/group/center-immigration-studies.

5. Spencer Nelson, "Hidden Clean Energy Gems," Clearpath, https://clearpath
.org/our-take/hidden-clean-energy-gems.

6. Anthony Adragna, "GOP Lawmaker: Green New Deal 'Tantamount to Genocide,'" *Politico*, March 14, 2019, https://www.politico.com/story/2019/03/14/green-new
-deal-genocide-1270839.

7. Andrew Sullivan, "It's Time to Resist the Excesses of #MeToo," *New York*, January 12, 2018, https://nymag.com/intelligencer/2018/01/andrew-sullivan-time-to-resist
-excesses-of-metoo.html.

8. Jonathan Chait, "The 'Shut It Down!' Left and the War on the Liberal Mind,"
New York, April 26, 2017, https://nymag.com/intelligencer/2017/04/the
-shut-it-down-left-and-the-war-on-the-liberal-mind.html.

9. Jessica Taylor, "Republican Cindy Hyde-Smith Wins Miss. Senate Runoff After
Racially Charged Campaign," National Public Radio, November 27, 2018, https://
www.npr.org/2018/11/27/671358332/republican-cindy-hyde-smith-wins-miss-senate
-runoff-after-racially-charged-campa.

10. James Arkin, "Hyde-Smith Apologizes 'to Anyone Offended' by Public Hanging Remark" *Politico*, November 20, 2018, https://www.politico.com/story/2018/11/20
/mississippi-debate-hyde-smith-espy-1009548.

11. Kara Gotsch and Vinay Basti, "Capitalizing on Mass Incarceration: U.S. Growth
in Private Prisons," Sentencing Project, August 2, 2018, https://www.sentencingproject
.org/publications/capitalizing-on-mass-incarceration-u-s-growth-in-private-prisons.

12. Derek Black and Eli Saslow, "How a Rising Star of White Nationalism Broke
Free from the Movement," interview by Terry Gross, *Fresh Air*, September 24, 2018,
https://www.npr.org/transcripts/651052970.

13. Christian Picciolini, "A Former Neo-Nazi Explains Why Hate Drew Him In—
and How He Got Out," interview by Dave Davies, *Fresh Air*, January 18, 2018, https://
www.npr.org/2018/01/18/578745514/a-former-neo-nazi-explains-why-hate-drew-him
-in-and-how-he-got-out.

14. Don Gonyea, "Majority of White Americans Say They Believe Whites Experience Discrimination," National Public Radio, October 24, 2017, https://www.npr.org
/2017/10/24/559604836/majority-of-white-americans-think-theyre-discriminated-against.

15. Greg Howard, "The Easiest Way to Get Rid of Racism? Just Redefine It," *New
York Times*, August 16, 2016, https://www.nytimes.com/2016/08/21/magazine/the
-easiest-way-to-get-rid-of-racism-just-redefine-it.html.

16. Charles Murray, "'The Bell Curve' 20 Years Later: A Q & A with Charles Murray," interview by Natalie Goodnow, American Enterprise Institute, October 16, 2014,
https://www.aei.org/economics/bell-curve-20-years-later-qa-charles-murray.

17. Murray, "'The Bell Curve' 20 Years Later."

18. Amanda E. Lewis and John B. Diamond, *Despite the Best Intentions: How Racial
Inequality Thrives in Good Schools* (New York: Oxford University Press, 2017), 176–78.

19. Murray, "'The Bell Curve' 20 Years Later."

20. Susan Glisson. "The Sum of Its Parts: The Importance of Deconstructing
Truth Commissions," *Race and Justice* (2015): 1–11.

21. Greensboro Truth and Reconciliation Commission, *Final Report*, http://www
.greensborotrc.org.

22. "Yale Retains Calhoun College's Name, Selects Names for Two New Residential Colleges, and Changes Title of 'Master' in the Residential Colleges," *YaleNews*,
April 27, 2016, https://news.yale.edu/2016/04/27/yale-retains-calhoun-college-s-name
-selects-names-two-new-residential-colleges-and-change.

23. Yuki Noguchi, "At Yale, Protests Mark a Fight to Recognize Union for Grad
Students," National Public Radio, June 16, 2017, https://www.npr.org/sections/ed/2017
/06/16/532774267/at-yale-protests-mark-a-fight-to-recognize-union-for-grad-students.

EPILOGUE

1. Nicole Chavez, Jason Hanna, Dakin Andone, and Madeline Holcombe, "Protesters Break Curfew on Another Night of Fury and Frustrations over George Floyd's
Killing," CNN, May 31, 2020, https://www.cnn.com/2020/05/30/us/george-floyd
-protests-saturday/index.html; Rebecca Tan, Marissa J. Lang, Antonio Olivo, Rachel
Chason, and John Woodrow Cox, "Night of Destruction Across D.C. After Protesters
Clash with Police Outside White House," *Washington Post*, June 1, 2020, https://www
.washingtonpost.com/local/dc-braces-for-third-day-of-protests-and-clashes-over-death
-of-george-floyd/2020/05/31/589471a4-a33b-11ea-b473-0490sb1af82b_story.html.

INDEX

ABOUT THE AUTHOR

Alex Zamalin is the director of the African American Studies Program and an assistant professor of political science at the University of Detroit Mercy. He is the author of numerous books, including, most recently, *Antiracism: An Introduction* and *Black Utopia: The History of an Idea from Black Nationalism to Afrofuturism*. Zamalin's essays and reviews have appeared in various edited book collections and in peer-reviewed journals such as *New Political Science*, *Contemporary Political Theory*, and *Political Theory*.